Greetings and
best wishes to Bill

Thoms' Friend, Mike
Radio —

J. F. Vium
8/26/87

W9-AHT-531

A Pretty Thin Salami

A Pretty Thin Salami

A History of the President's Salary

by
James F. Vivian

VANTAGE PRESS
New York / Washington / Atlanta
Los Angeles / Chicago

FIRST EDITION

All rights reserved, including the right of
reproduction in whole or in part in any form.

Copyright © 1987 by James F. Vivian

Published by Vantage Press, Inc.
516 West 34th Street, New York, New York 10001

Manufactured in the United States of America
ISBN: 0-533-07056-2

Library of Congress Catalog Card No.: 86-90106

For Diane

Contents

Preface   ix

1. Washington   1
2. Grant   19
3. Roosevelt   35
4. The Last Tax-exempt President   51
5. Truman and Johnson   73
6. Conclusion   95

Index   103

Preface

Books and studies of the American presidency are plentiful. Recently a retired businessman, long fascinated by the subject, publicized a private collection of more than 1,300 works. They deal with the president as an institution, leader, administrator, commander-in-chief, diplomat, interpreter, innovator, legislator, enforcer, orator, and many more aspects. Others treat the presidents' health, religion, pastimes, families, and even pets. In the last generation it has become intriguing to ponder the process by which presidential aspirants are culled, nominated, and elected. Still other books are devoted to the succession, whether of another elected person or the vice-president. A few of these books are anecdotal, relishing the presidents' sense of humor or, more recently, probing their personalities. And, of course, every president has been credited with at least one major, documented biography. Of late, a comparable, if belated, interest has been shown in the presidents' wives.

Curiously, however, there is no study available of the president's salary—its determination, evolution, and contemporary disposition. The present work represents an effort in that direction. The word *effort* is used advisedly, because to speak of the salary is also necessarily in part to consider the emoluments, perquisites, and privileges attached to the office, no matter how elusive and disparate these may be. To speak of the salary is also sometimes to allude to the presidents' personal assets, no matter how uncertain and awkward this frequently is. And finally, to speak of the salary is unavoidably to risk an ideal, no matter how brash and presumptuous it appears.

But these hazards need not impede the goal, which is to examine who, when, and how the president's salary has been decided. To that end, this study is imperatively partly a composite of previous findings extracted from biographical sources, partly a synthesis of scattered topical information, and partly a product of original research. If something of the results can be reasonably anticipated—namely, that the president's salary is historically less than a munificent sum—there are other points developed that are less manifest and some that may prove revealing. Certainly the whole should allow for a special insight into the national attitude toward its highest elective office and, in the process, elaborate the shifting estimates the public ascribes to the position and to those who have occupied it.

My indebtedness to others for their assistance, advice, and encouragement is admitted freely. Professors Stephen C. Markovich and Theodore Pedeliski of the department of political science at the University of North Dakota reviewed important segments of the material and offered instructive critical suggestions. Professor Bonniejean Christensen of the department of English of the University of North Dakota and Dr. John D. Macoll, of the Department of Agriculture, Washington, D.C., read the draft manuscript for style and continuity. The staff at the Chester Fritz Library at the University of North Dakota, especially the resourceful personnel in the interlibrary loan branch, patiently endured my many requests. And my wife, Diane, never withheld her endearing friendship, confidence, and support. All missteps, oversights, and infelicities are, of course, my responsibility entirely.

A Pretty Thin Salami

1
Washington

The president of the United States receives a regular, prescribed salary. The salary, which is secured by the Constitution, commences upon formal inauguration and ceases upon departure from office. It has been so since George Washington first took the oath of office on April 30, 1789. Although the idea of a presidential salary won a constitutional protection in 1789, the guarantee shortly formed a cage from which escape has proven infrequent and difficult. There have been only four revisions of the salary in more than 200 years. A favorable combination of circumstances has been necessary in each instance, not alone because of certain stipulated restrictions. Additionally, unexpected developments and consequences have been the rule, so that the subject now affords a poorly appreciated opportunity to explore the progress of an institutional experience whose history is still unfolding.

The question of whether or not to pay the president a salary arose early in the proceedings at the constitutional convention in Philadelphia in 1787. At the time, some state governors, including those of Virginia, New York, and Massachusetts, received a salary for their services. The Virginia Constitution specified "an adequate, but moderate salary," while Massachusetts assured its

1

governors an "honorable" and "fixed" salary. Other states provided a salary but ensconced the principle in language cautioning prudence in the disbursement of public monies to government officials and employees. Still other governors received no salary at all, except that their official expenses, in whole or in part, were met from the state's treasury.[1]

At the Philadelphia convention, none argued the need for a presidential salary more stoutly than Alexander Hamilton of New York, probably the strongest champion of a vigorous, independent executive. "It is impossible to imagine any provision," he wrote, "which would have been more eligible than this" for categorical insertion in the Constitution. Without it, Hamilton contended, the legislative authority, when exercising its power of the purse, might be tempted to influence the presidency and even intrude directly upon its prerogatives and responsibilities. (Doubtless he remembered the device developed during the colonial era, when salary amendments attached to important legislation sometimes forced stubborn royal governors to negotiate an amicable compromise.) An established rule, said Hamilton, was frankly necessary to prevent "the intimidation or seduction of the executive by the terrors, or allurements, of the pecuniary arrangements" decided by Congress. Adoption of the principle would bolster the president's resoluteness, Hamilton believed, and lessen the prospect of his integrity being corrupted and fortitude weakened. Hamilton could not "commend too highly the judicious attention which has been paid to this subject."[2]

Two contrary views proved less persuasive. Everyday "wages" should apply to public servants, one critic wrote, if only to remind them of their employers' prerogatives and "to put a stop to the impertinence of individuals in asking for high salaries." Thus a congressman deserved not more than five dollars per day, a senator six dollars, and the president seven dollars, "with an allowance for his table." Benjamin Franklin, another, more thoughtful critic, objected to providing executive salaries or stipends of any kind. Such salaries proposed to fuse motives of avarice and ambition into a single "tempestuous" passion that from his long experience and observations had been all too prevalent in Great Britain and its empire. To make the presidency at once the locus of power and profit risked "the most violent effects." Better, he thought, to keep the office one of honor and distinction, although adequately sustained in privileges and perquisites. Hamilton himself seconded Franklin's motion, less for its "practicability," he said, than out of respect for its seasoned author.[3]

The minority changed few minds, partly because both the Virginia and New Jersey plans for constitutional revision rejected their view.[4] Hamilton's concept prevailed easily, leading to a fundamental guarantee with the ratification of the Constitution in 1789. The president of the United States, unlike the president of Congress under the supplanted Articles of Confederation adopted in 1781, was to be an annually salaried officer of government. In addition, the salary, once fixed, would remain constant for the whole of any president's four-year term.

This meant a break with the recent past. Franklin's view in particular comported closely with the practice begun in 1774 and continued until Washington's inauguration. Sympathy for it forced a modification in the Hamiltonian consensus sufficient to prohibit the states, separately or in combination, from granting the president any benefits or allowances supplementary to the salary.[5] As a result, Article II, Section 1, of the finished Constitution, when published and subsequently ratified, stipulated that: "The President shall, at stated Times, receive for his Services a Compensation, which shall neither be increased nor diminished during the Period for which he shall have been elected, and he shall not receive within that Period any other Emolument from the United States, or any of them."

The clause was first applied to Washington. His fourteen titular predecessors, the presidents of Congress, were chosen from among the delegates in Congress to preside over its deliberations and affairs. None enjoyed a salary by virtue of the distinction and honor bestowed upon him, irrespective of irregular lengths of tenure. Whatever payment each received came as a delegate only, provided by the state he represented and usually on a per diem basis. The duties included overseeing official correspondence and entertaining worthy guests and dignitaries. Some presidents of Congress performed more willingly and capably than others. Most found their expenses in meeting the random obligations and expectations in excess of the allowance granted by Congress, starting in 1779. For the wealthy presidents, like John Hancock, the difference was discounted to public service. For the less fortunate, like Samuel Huntington, an adjustment became advisable. Gradually a consensus emerged that the government should defray the president's official expenses in their totality, including home rental, steward, clerk, and livery. Private and personal expenses, as denoted by the Articles of Confederation, remained an uncompensated, individual responsibility.[6]

The cost of these amenities and perquisites varied importantly and typically toward higher sums, even allowing for the steep currency depreciation of the decade. In the mid-1780s Congress balked at continuing the practice of virtually unlimited reimbursements, first by demanding greater efficiency and accountability, then by capping the total at a stated maximum. A ceiling of $10,000–$12,000 seems to have been widely agreed upon when Congress sighted the shoals, if not of outright bankruptcy, certainly of "degrading poverty." "Even the small pittance necessary for the subsistence of the President's household, in the most eligible style of republican neatness and simplicity," one delegate reported to his state's governor, "[is] only attainable from other inadequate appropriations."[7] At this point the founding fathers drafted a new form of government whose constitution featured a guaranteed compensation to the chief executive. Since the guarantee in Article II established a principle, not an actual amount, the First Congress convened under the ratified document soon set about to supply the numbers.

This was done through the summer of 1789, beginning in May with the appointment of a select committee to study the presidential and other salary questions. Serious debate on the committee's report, which recommended between $20,000 and $30,000 per year, began in mid July. The committee itself inclined to the lesser of the two amounts, but its chairman conceded that the recommendation represented the majority view between the extremes of $15,000 and $70,000. Much depended, said the chairman, on the style and decorum one anticipated for the president, and whether an expense allowance would supplement the salary. Except for the experience of the former presidents of Congress, whose expenses he noted had ranged from $7,000 to $13,000 annually, there was little information on which to proceed. Establishing any sum would necessarily involve a crude projection.[8]

Tobias Lear, Washington's diligent private secretary since 1786, compiled a statement at about this time listing the president's expenses for the opening eleven weeks of the administration. These amounted to $3,656, not including rental on the second, larger house in New York City, some furniture and firewood, all of which Washington paid for personally. This sum, extended forward for the whole of 1789, yielded an estimated total of $17,282. The projection may then have been passed to the House select committee for its information and guidance. Regardless, Washington behaved not too differently than his predecessors. He refused the promised salary in his inaugural address on April 30, as he also had payment for military services rendered during the Revolutionary War, and further proposed limiting "the pecuniary estimates" of the presidency "to such actual expenditures as the public good may be thought to require." In office, Washington permitted his expenses to climb without giving too much heed to cost, convinced that the president's surroundings should impart "respectability." Although admittedly "indispensable," he said, the presidential salary pertained mostly to his successors, less directly to himself.[9]

Yet, in the House of Representatives, a problem in constitutional interpretation arose, the first of many to follow on the subject: Should the guarantee of compensation to the president and the prohibition against further emoluments be taken in combination or handled separately? That is, was the compensation to mean a total of both salary and official expenses, or were expenses distinguishable from emoluments? The House, on the motion of another member, decided for the former interpretation. Compensation and emoluments would be treated as one. In providing the president with $25,000 annually, the House intended that the sum represent both a salary and also expenses presumably sufficient to cover household and official needs. The home purchased in April, 1790, for the president in the temporary capital at Philadelphia, together with the furniture placed in it, would remain public property. All other official and personal expenses the president would be obliged to pay for from the proposed $25,000 yearly appropriation. Washington and at least fifteen successors were completely at liberty to choose how many secretaries, maids and valets, and domestics they desired—or could afford.[10]

In the sequence of affairs, Congress had simply carried forward its experience with the costs of the presidency under the old order, perhaps $10,000–$15,000 annually, to which it appended a salary increment of about $10,000. Consequently, no other official compensation even approximated that assigned the executive. Those were decided as a simple question of salary, without any other than nominal privileges. The vice-president was granted $5,000 annually. Everyone else, including Cabinet officers and judges at all ranks, received still less. The major exceptions, themselves suggestive, were the diplomatic ministers appointed to the royal courts in London and Paris, each of whom received an annual salary of $9,000 plus an allowance of $4,000 for housing, wardrobe and entertainment.[11]

Upon defeating two attempts to lower the president's compensation to $20,000 and to raise the vice-president's to $6,000, the Senate effected no change in the House action. The measure, as finally adopted in midSeptember, 1789, passed in the character determined by the larger chamber. President Washington signed it on September 24. "As he means not to apply any part of [the $25,000] to his own emolument, and will expend no more than he finds requisite," Congressman James Madison reassured a friend, "the allowance is of an experimental nature. It was necessary to ensure a sufficiency. During his administration the proper sum to be made permanent will be discovered."[12]

Not two days later, however, the unexpected occurred, at least for one skeptical senator, when a colleague introduced an account of $8,000 for repairs and appointments to the president's residence. "This was a great surprise to me," Pennsylvania's senator William Maclay confided to his diary, "for although a vote had originated in the House . . . for furnishing the house, yet I considered the allowance for all this had been made in the President's salary."[13]

Administrative expenses, notably official salaries, counted among the many points of growing contention. On the one side there were those who argued that adequate salaries attracted abler persons to public service and rendered corruption less likely. These seem to have been the people who set the agenda and largely influenced the initial salary schedules. On the other side there were those, like Maclay, who objected to the tendency toward higher outlays by a government supposedly founded on the principles of simplicity and thrift. High salaries, they believed, whetted private interest and threatened the centralization of federal authority. Public servants generally received too much; congressmen needed not more than two dollars a day, unless they desired to profit from their positions; and the president's salary could be expediently halved without damage or embarrassment.[14]

Although slow to organize an opposition, the critics were better prepared by 1793. The House then not only "spent some time" discussing the bill to reauthorize the president's salary and rejecting the "several" unspecified amendments to it, but also defeated by a slim six-vote margin a motion to limit the appropriation to four years, "and no more." The attack mounted the following year was even more frontal. Congressman Thomas Tredwell of New York introduced a resolution seeking to reduce the salary at the close of Washington's second term by more than half, to $12,000 annually. Connecticut representative Jeremiah Wadsworth's withering sarcasm, about flagrantly pandering to popular favor to win reelection, forced its voluntary and speedy withdrawal.[15]

Differences remained unresolved when in 1796 they were aggravated anew, abetted in part by the emergence of political parties of conflicting persuasions. Early in the year Congress took up the challenge of how to fund the construction of the federal capital buildings in the District of Columbia without assuming a direct liability and risk in the commitment. In the end, after much imaginative exploring and some conscious evasion, the House agreed to authorize the District commissioners appointed in 1790 to negotiate a loan redeemable upon the sale of lots in the preserve, and to designate the president the principal agent in the business. All this opened the discussion to the status of the Capitol and White House, neither of which had progressed very far toward completion and the scheduled removal there of the government at the turn of the century.[16]

It seems that $97,000 had been spent thus far in constructing the White House and $80,000 appropriated toward erecting the Capitol. A total of $700,000, probably more, was thought necessary to finish both edifices. Lofty as these sums sounded to nearly everyone interested, to some they loomed as plainly exorbitant. Connecticut's Joshua Coit held that a building costing $50,000 would be fully adequate for the president's house. "Gentlemen might talk of elegance, of splendor and magnificence," he declared, "but in the present state of the [national] finances . . . more attention should be paid to use and economy." Others, like Henry Dearborn of Massachusetts, suggested that the unfinished White House, which even some of the president's friends felt overly large, might

9

yet be adapted as the Capitol or placed at the disposal of the Supreme Court, with another, smaller unit built nearby for the chief executive.[17]

The relevancy to the president's salary and perquisites became evident when Washington, in the eighth State of the Union address in December, 1796, counseled toward its close that the "compensations of the officers of the United States," particularly in the "most important stations, appear to call for legislative revision." Low salaries dulled the attractiveness of these positions, he advised, leaving government to draw from a shallow pool of talent. Moreover, Washington observed, "it would be repugnant to the vital principles of our Government virtually to exclude from public trusts talents and virtues unless accompanied by wealth."[18] The full extent of Congress's obligations, current and prospective, now emerged in bold relief. They included, in addition to the question of official salaries generally, the presidential salary, the expenses of the presidency, and the "palace" then building in the permanent capital. As to basic administrative costs and expenses, events, trends, and recommendations had converged to beckon the beginnings of resolution.

Congressional reaction to Washington's appeal came in two forms: directly, in a bill to increase official salaries, and indirectly, in a motion to accommodate the president in added household comforts. The issue of the president's salary intervened obliquely, on a motion to augment the measure on official salaries. The upshot of the combined debate and resolution of its several parts was to establish, at the insistence of one vocal congressman and his allies, an unstated rule destined to hold sway for many decades to come.

The question of whether to raise official salaries reached the floor first. Proponents argued earnestly that the quality and compentency of government would suffer should the bill fail. Perhaps their best points dealt with the difficulty the president experienced in filling some positions, the discrimination inherently involved with inadequate salaries amid expensive living conditions, and the virtual exclusion of hopeful applicants from distant states where incomes averaged distinctly less than in urban centers. Rumors circulated meanwhile that some resignations, notably Alexander Hamilton's as secretary of treasury, had been owing to the low salary.[19]

Alternately, opponents pointed to the critical state of the nation's finances, recurring international tensions, and declining foreign commerce as powerful justifications for deferring consideration of the matter. "Public officers must submit to bear a share of the evils in common with others," announced John Nicholas of Virginia.[20]

By and large, the critics carried the day, whittling down the several parts of the bill by refusing the special consideration proposed for some officials or by blocking efforts to adopt incremental increases for all. Although some lesser public servants and certain of those assigned throughout the states received favorable concessions, the main body of government officers had to settle for a 25 percent across-the-board adjustment without distinction. The so-called rule of parsimony continued inviolate.[21]

Meantime, Congress began considering the merits of two bills to raise the president's and vice president's salaries by $5,000 and $2,000 respectively and to appropriate $14,000 for new furniture in the president's house. The Senate passed both bills in February, 1797, the second by an overwhelming majority. As for the first bill, the Senate had originated it in keeping with the agreement of 1789 to review the adequacy of official salaries after the experience of Washington's tenure. The committee appointed in the House to study the matter reported against the increase. This immediately prompted a move to postpone debate on the bill to March 4. A new presidential term would have commenced on that date, triggering the constitutional prohibition against altering the president's compensation while in office. Although the motion failed by a single vote, it strongly indicated that the House would defeat the bill no matter how lengthy the ensuing debate.[22]

Two members, John Williams of New York and Daniel Buck of Vermont, nevertheless spoke eloquently in support of the bill. Williams, reminding his colleagues of his appointment to the committee examining official salaries, noted that it had found the president's compensation inadequate to enable him "to live in a style becoming his situation." Buck expressed his confidence in the good sense of the people and the promise of the national experiment in federalism. True, the president's salary of $25,000 "had a great sound in the ears of many," but after looking "into the reason of the thing," he concluded that it fell short of the requirements and duties of the office. He believed others would agree upon inspection, and that Americans were disposed to provide a proper support.[23]

Happily, said Buck, Washington was "a man of fortune" who had spent the salary on the enhancement of the presidency without any suggestion of ostentation or waste. Would this be the usual case, he wondered, intimating that he knew Washington typically committed another $5,000 yearly from his own assets. Were Americans "always to expect to have a president who gives his service to the country?" Buck thought not. If no increase was voted, he said, future presidents would hesitate to "come forward to support the same style . . . [if it meant] infringing on their own fortunes."[24]

Much the same could be said of the vice president and other government officials, Buck continued. None had any right to enrich themselves at the public expense, he recognized, but they should enjoy "a handsome living" while in office. He believed that the people were able and willing to provide for the reasonable expenses of their government and that the recently increased salaries approved in some states for legislators and officials indicated it.[25]

But Robert Rutherford of Virginia thought the proposition "altogether improper and unjust." It smacked of royalism and the splendors of "kings, priests, and courts." The habit of "simplicity" and "plainness of manners" needed constant reinforcement if a "happy people" were to be confirmed in their virtues. Patriotism, declared Rutherford, "could not be purchased." No one need despair that failure to increase the salary would produce a vacant presidency, or that the government might be driven to hire an incumbent. Rather, said Rutherford, "there would always be found men of abilities and patriotism to fill that office, without any view to pecuniary advantage."[26]

George Dent of Maryland asked if the question was divisible. He favored raising the president's salary by $5,000 but not the vice president's by $2,000. The chair ruled against him. This was followed by a motion to delete the clause relating to the vice presidency, which was adopted.[27]

Returning to the central theme, both Robert Goodloe Harper of South Carolina and John Page of Virginia voiced their vehement objections to a higher presidential salary. Harper thought the proposed $5,000 raise more beneficially applied to the welfare of members of the House and Senate, some of whom subsisted in their capacities on meager margins. Page believed that the bill concealed a "mischievous tendency" which could only bode

13

ill while the country faced parlous and straitened conditions. Better to retrench and possibly to suffer the loss of a "good officer," he felt, then to risk having to levy stiffer taxes among the populace. Harper and Page numbered among the fifty-eight–member majority that overwhelmed the bill's thirty-eight defenders. The rejection sounded of finality. Supportive sentiment virtually collapsed, and prospects for resurrecting the bill dissipated completely.[28]

The House bill to authorize $14,000 for furniture for the president's house definitely fared better, if to a larger point. As some members observed, the precedents dating back to 1779, renewed with the creation of the new government, were strong in support of the measure. The institutional presidency, as opposed to its interim occupant, should be sustained at public expense, they believed, despite the constitutional prohibition against granting emoluments during a given term. True, about $13,000 had been spent in 1789 to furnish the president's household. But the bill at hand contemplated replacing both the worn and dilapidated stock and purchasing acquisitions preparatory to the removal of the capital to the Federal District. To that end, the reporting committee calculated $14,000 reasonable for the purpose. Half that amount, as one or two members argued, would hardly suffice if the appearance and facilities of the president's official residence mattered at all.[29]

One critic, however, pressed the debate to a policy conclusion. Nathaniel Macon of South Carolina felt the time opportune to establish a basic principle—specifically, that Congress could not provide for both the president and the president's household, as thus far had been the case, regardless of the supposed settlement arrived at in 1789. Speaking personally, Macon preferred that the president's salary "be the only consideration . . . for his services." The president had been guaranteed quite "an ample salary." At the least it should prove adequate to ending the inherited practice, Macon contended, of also defraying his expenses.[30]

By a vote of 63–27, newly inaugurated President John Adams got the $14,000 with which to replace and improve the furnishings of his rude official household (not all of which he spent), but not an increase in salary. In the process Congress also affirmed its preference for subscribing the perquisites of the presidency, however modestly and sometimes reluctantly, rather than trusting to the resources and inclination of its occupant. The precedents earlier established on this score were recovered and renewed in lieu of salary adjustments lest parts and aspects of the office become a species of private property. President Thomas Jefferson took occupancy of the White House in 1801 already armed with a sheaf of sketched structural improvements and architectural innovations, which Congress paid for. Four years later, over Congressman Macon's fervent objections, Congress also authorized Jefferson to sell the worn furniture and to apply the proceeds to a $14,000 appropriation for new stock. There was no call to review the president's salary, which Jefferson found inadequate by $3,000–$4,000 throughout his first administration, despite his careful accounting of expenditures. Macon had warned against it. The salary, already august, he deposed, would never compare to the "elegant" surroundings.[31]

An undeclared compromise had been effected. The critics succeeded in serving a kind of notice that no one, particularly the incumbent, should expect a presidential salary different from the one provided. The $25,000 entered into the statutes by the First Congress became decidedly fixed, with the result that in short order, it acquired the attributes of an extraconstitutional rule only slightly less deeply etched than the guarantee clause contained in Article II. Since the guarantee of salary could not be eliminated except by the difficult process of amendment, so too would the actual amount achieve a comparable status. The two elements—the guarantee and its stipulated amount—assumed a synonymous identity under terms that restricted the president's ability to separate them. Sixty years later, the Confederate States of America accepted both as a constant. The provisional government, created in the spring of 1861, authorized its president the same salary of $25,000, and the permanent constitution, ratified the following December, duplicated to the letter the guarantee clause in the repudiated Constitution of 1789.[32]

Hamilton had secured the salaried independence of the executive, yet implicitly conceded Congress sole power to determine its real worth, most probably during the interregnum between administrations. Moreover, faced with an exigency to distinguish between salary and expenses and perquisites, Congress only briefly considered all three equally and together. Soon it reverted to the familiar practice of concentrating on institutional expenses and perquisites. Except for furnishings and sundry allied amenities, the president's salary came to mean the balance of $25,000 after his other personal needs and expenses had been satisfied, according to taste, habits and circumstances. "The representatives of the people [are] the sole arbitors of the public expense," Jefferson wrote, "and do not permit any work [or disbursements] to be forced on them on a larger scale than their judgment deems adapted to the circumstances of the Nation."[33]

President Adams, Washington's successor and a person of modest means, became the first real test of the working arrangement. He fared poorly almost from the start, writing his wife early in his administration of the heavy expenses involved in maintaining himself in office. He wondered if he might not be "obliged to resign in six months." "I can't live" within the allotted income, he confided. At least seven succeeding presidents experienced similar discouragement and hardship without evoking any serious concern from Congress on the adequacy of the prescribed salary.[34]

1. Joseph E. Kallenbach, *The American Chief Executive: The Presidency and the Governorship* (New York: Harper and Row, 1966), 195–96.

2. Max Beloff, ed., *The Federalist* (Oxford: Blackwell, 1948), 374.

3. Morton Borden, ed., *The Antifederalist Papers* (Lansing: Michigan State University Press, 1965), 33–34; Ronald W. Clark, *Benjamin Franklin: A Biography* (New York: Random House, 1983), 408–09; Harold E. Syrett, ed., *The Papers of Alexander Hamilton* (New York: Columbia University Press, 1962), Vol. 4, 176–77.

4. Kallenbach, *American Chief Executives,* 196–97.

5. Ibid.; Jeffrey Tullis, "On Presidential Character," in *The Presidency in the Constitutional Order,* ed. Joseph M. Bessette and Jeffrey Tullis (Baton Rouge: Louisiana State University Press, 1981), 286–87.

6. Edmund C. Burnett, "Perquisites of the President of the Continental Congress," *American Historical Review* 35 (October 1929): 69–76; Jennings B. Sanders, *The Presidency of the Continental Congress,* 1774–1789, Rev. ed. (Gloucester: Peter Smith, 1971) 44–52. President Henry Laurens was asked in January, 1779, to submit a statement of expenditures. His honestly flustered reply is contained in Paul H. Smith, ed., *Letters of Delegates to Congress, 1774—89* (Washington, D.C.: Library of Congress, 1985), Vol. 11, 497–98.

7. Edmund C. Burnett, ed., *Letters of Members of the Continental Congress* (Washington, D.C.: Carnegie Institute, 1936), Vol. 8, 696.

8. *Debates and Proceedings of the Congress of the U.S.,* 1789–91, 645–46.

9. Douglas S. Freeman, *George Washington: A Biography* (New York: Charles Scribner's Sons, 1954), Vol. 6, 225, 252; U.S. House of Representatives, *Inaugural Addresses of the Presidents of the United States,* 89th Cong., 1st sess., 1965, House Doc. 51, 3–4; and William A. DeGregorio, *The Complete Book of U.S. Presidents* (New York: Dembner Books, 1984), 14, which contains useful summaries of wills and bequests.

10. *Debates and Proceedings of the Congress of the U.S.,* 1789–91, 634–36; Allan L. Damon, "Presidential Expenses," *American Heritage* 25 (June 1974): 64–65.

11. *American State Papers,* I. *(Miscellaneous)* 34: 57.

12. *Debates and Proceedings of the Congress of the U.S.,* 1789–91, 57–9; Charles F. Hobson and Robert A. Rutland, eds., *Papers of James Madison* (Charlottesville: University Press of Virginia, 1979), Vol. 12, 295.

13. Edgar S. Maclay, ed., *Journal of William Maclay* (New York: D. Appleton and Co., 1890), 166.

14. Ibid., 74; Donald H. Stewart, *The Opposition Press of the Federalist Period* (Albany: State University Press of New York, 1969), 71–7.

15. *Annals of Congress,* 2d Cong., 1791–93, 866–67; ibid., 3d Cong., 1793–95, 782.

16. Ibid., 4th Cong., 1st Sess., 1795–96, 366–68, 374–75, 826–40; John C. Miller, *The Federalist Era,* 1789–1801 (New York: Harper and Bros., 1960), 252.

17. *Annals of Congress,* 4th Cong., 1st Sess., 1795–96, 374, 827.

18. Leonard D. White, *The Federalists* (New York: Macmillan, 1948), 291.

19. Ibid., 292–93.

20. Ibid.; *Annals of Congress,* 4th Cong., 2d Sess., 1796–97, 2002.

21. *Annals of Congress,* 4th Cong., 2d Sess., 1796–97, 2000–12.

22. Ibid., 2090–92.

23. Ibid., 2100–1.

24. Ibid., 2101; James T. Flexner, *George Washington and the New Nation,* 1783–1793 (Boston: Little, Brown and Co., 1970), 202.

25. *Annals of Congress,* 4th Cong., 2d Sess., 1796–97, 2101–2.

26. Ibid., 2104.

27. Ibid., 2103–4.

28. Ibid., 2104–5.

29. Ibid., 2307–20.

30. Ibid.

31. *Annals of Congress,* 6th Cong., 1799–1801, 1068–71; William Ryan and Desmond Guinness, *The White House: An Architectural History* (New York: McGraw-Hill Co., 1980), 93, 122, 106–08; U.S. House of Representatives, *Journal,* 8th Cong., 2d Sess., 1804–5, 388–9; Noble E. Cunningham, Jr., *The Process of Government under Jefferson* (Princeton: Princeton University Press, 1978), 44–45.

32. James M. Matthews, ed., *Statutes at Large of the Provisional Government of the Confederate States of America* (Richmond, Va.: R. M. Smith, 1864), 63–4; Charles R. Lee, Jr., *The Confederate Constitutions* (Chapel Hill: University of North Carolina Press, 1963), 165. The vice president and Cabinet officers were paid $6,000 each.

33. Damon, "Presidential Expenses," 65; Ryan and Guinness, eds., *The White House,* 108.

34. Henry F. Graff, "The Wealth of the Presidents," *American Heritage,* Vol. 17 (October 1966), 4–5, 106–11.

2
Grant

The presidential salary did indeed remain fixed—for the next seventy-five years. The institution changed in the meanwhile, of course, growing slowly to embrace a staff of White House groundskeepers, watchmen, and maintenance personnel. Perhaps the most substantive of these changes occurred in 1857. With the politically divided Thirty-fourth Congress rushing to clear its agenda before dispersing, Democratic senator Richard Brodhead of Pennsylvania offered an amendment to the civil appropriations bill to provide the president at public expense with a secretary, steward, and two messengers. The House accepted it without objection. The finished bill passed the same day it was submitted, on the eve of President James Buchanan's inauguration.[1]

But the salary continued as originally decided. There had been no effort to revise it after 1797; and congressional discussion on the successful motion in 1853 to raise the vice president's salary by $3,000, together with those of Cabinet officers, at no time generated any comment on the president's.[2] In fact, when the question of the president's salary next surfaced, it happened only because of an amendment latterly attached to an ordinary housekeeping budget, intentionally designed as well to benefit many others in government. The president appears personally to have played no part in activating the idea, even though the episode, certainly in its outline and conclusion, it is today the single best known of the revisions.

The annual legislative, executive, and judicial appropriations bill had been introduced in the House of Representatives in early December 1872, slightly more than a month after President U. S. Grant won election to his second term. Debate followed intermittently. On January 8, 1873, Republican congressman Aaron A. Sargent of California moved an amendment which, among other points, proposed to double the president's salary to $50,000. Democratic congressman William S. Holman of Indiana, already cultivating the reputation of a vigilant watchdog guarding the Treasury portals, quickly objected on the grounds that the motion constituted new legislation requiring separate treatment and that, in any event, the salary had been permanently fixed in law. Chairman James A. Garfield of the Appropriations Committee, with the support of the House Majority, sustained Holman's point of order. The bill in its entirety, minus Sargent's suggested amendment, passed on January 15.[3]

The Senate afterward added several amendments of its own to the bill. The House took up the measure again on February 24 when only a week remained before final adjournment. Garfield, floor manager of the bill by virtue of his committee chairmanship, hoped to expedite a routine enactment. He was shortly disappointed and, worse, placed in an awkward position whose potential embarrassments included the reaction of an outraged constituency.

House debate had no sooner begun when Republican congressman Benjamin F. Butler of Massachusetts moved to amend further a Senate amendment relating to the salaries of certain clerks and others employed by Congress. Butler's amendment proposed nothing less than a comprehensive upward revision of the whole federal salary structure, beginning with the president and vice president and ending with Congress itself, for an estimated total of $1.2 million in increased expenditures. Parts of the amendment also envisioned a retroactive application of some provisions to March 1871, or to the start of the Republican-dominated Forty-second Congress, thereby awarding every incumbent member with a bonus of $5,000.[4]

After contending with another procedural challenge, Garfield willingly opened the floor to a ranging consideration of a subject that had been simmering since the inflation due to the Civil War had effectively eroded the value of fixed salaries by an average one-third. Attempts at selective interim adjustments, notably in 1866, 1868, and 1869, had met with limited s[.] ·ness.[5] Congressional and certain judicial salaries had been increased slightly, but not so most others. The stage had been set for the famous (or infamous) "salary grab" of the Gilded Age, even as Congress had yet to recover its credibility concerning other "scandalous" instances of alleged venality and fraud.

The bill may have been ethically dubious but not, as some charged, illegal. It passed the House handily. The Senate thereupon balked at certain of its newly attached features, approving some and rejecting the rest. In the end, after an extended Sunday meeting of the designated conference committees reconciled the disputed points, the bill passed both chambers just hours before the session expired. The House had successfully imposed its salaries measure on the hesitant upper chamber. Garfield had avoided the very real prospect of an extended session which would have stalled some twenty million dollars in needed appropriations. But in so doing he brought down upon himself a "carnival of calumny" for responsibly retaining control of his legislative obligation.[6]

President Grant signed the bill on March 3, the same day it passed Congress and on the eve of his inauguration to a second term. Earlier, on February 29, Garfield had occasion to visit the White House. The bill entered into the conversation. Grant, whose family enjoyed receiving guests and holding frequent receptions, confided to Garfield that unless it passed, he would be "compelled four years hence to draw at least $25,000 out of his private property to enable him to leave town."[7] The president realized a doubled salary beginning on March 4, 1873, not because of the popularity of the idea, but because of a majority of Congress irrespective of party determined themselves deserving of increased compensation and travel allowances. In fact, had the weighty amendment been divided into its many parts and each voted separately, as Garfield originally desired, the provision to raise the president's salary would have likely failed.

The comments uttered in debate bore this out. Butler confessed his initial skepticism and a reluctance to sponsor the bill, until it became clear that Congress had been derelict in recent years in advancing the same level of expenses and support as before, even allowing for the belated renovations lately accomplished in the debilitated official residence. Two minutely detailed inventories, both of which were ordered published in the *Congressional Record,* supplied the evidence and dramatized the contrast in the contents and comforts of the Executive Mansion between 1801 and 1869. These lists, coupled with the knowledge that the intrinsic value of the salary had been seriously reduced during the intervening 70 years, convinced Butler that an important upward revision was overdue.[8]

Constitutional interpretation formed the nub of the first and stoutest challenge after some procedural questions had been satisfied. The amendment, said Republican congressman John F. Farnsworth of Illinois, begged the problem of how Article II was to be applied in the case of a president who, like Grant, had been reelected but not reinaugurated. That is, did the presidential term begin upon election or inauguration? No answer was immediately forthcoming before a colleague, Horatio C. Burchard, also an Illinois Republican, seconded opposition to the measure. The mutual independence of the legislative and executive branches, said Burchard, implied a corollary preventing the president from exercising "the influence of his official position to increase his own salary." The prospect of a president signing the bill to raise the prescribed salary "violated the spirit of the Constitution," which, if permitted to occur, should result in his impeachment.[9]

The clause invited solicitude, Farnsworth admitted. Yet, every previous president seemed to have found the salary "sufficient." Abraham Lincoln saved $50,000 of it over four years when the price of gold soared by 250 percent. In addition, Congress cooperatively funded emoluments and "various other things" that not even $50,000 could buy in the marketplace: "We provide . . . everything except his provisions; and we provide even a part of those, for we furnish his garden and gardeners; we furnish all his furniture; we furnish his stables, recently rebuilt at a cost of $30,000. We furnish nearly all of his servants, all his clerks and secretaries, his gas and fuel . . ." Any debate of the proposal was beside the point, Burchard insisted. To alter the salary in these circumstances still amounted to a technical violation of the Constitution, by "passing the bill on the third of March and make it take effect of the fourth of March."[10]

Two congressmen rose to the bill's defense. One, Clarkson N. Potter, a New York Democrat, justified his support on the basis that all government officers were entitled to higher salaries than they currently received. Even with the suggested increase, for example, the president would still realize "a less compensation than the salary . . . paid to the first president," after living expenses had been adjusted. Sargent of California, author of the original amendment to raise the salary, referred to the examination he had conducted. It showed the president to be "meanly paid," Sargent said, and he doubted anyone could arrive at a different conclusion by the same process. In fact, he suggested, it seemed quite likely that Grant had dipped into his personal reserves during the past four years, perhaps equivalent to a whole year's salary, in order to meet the obligations of the office and what others expected of him. The "injustice" needed correcting, preferably soon enough that Grant himself could benefit from it.[11]

In the end the bill passed by the narrow margin of 102–96, and then at the threat of an extra session if agreement could not be reached within the waning minutes prior to final adjournment.

The Senate was much more sympathetically inclined to raising the president's salary, despite the vehement opposition of two members who promised to accomplish its defeat by whatever means available. Opposition to the measure hinged on the comprehensiveness of the proposal on salaries generally, under conditions limiting analytical debate and holding compulsory legislation hostage to its resolution. For that reason, Senator Edmunds of Vermont offered an amendment to separate the question of the presidential salary from the omnibus bill. Other salaries, he noted, could be considered at comparative leisure, whereas the Constitution allowed only for a specific opportunity to revise the president's salary.[12]

Edmunds's motion failed less because of its demerits than because it projected a second lengthy conference committee session between the two houses, risking the suspension of more immediate matters. Likewise the motion by Republican senator George G. Wright of Iowa. He remained unalterably opposed to any and all salary increases, even to the point of refusing to cooperate with the conference committee's report. As in the House, the appropriations bill, including the salaries amendment, passed narrowly by 36–27. There were more members absent by one than accounted for the difference between those who favored and rejected the bill.[13]

Several senators and congressmen rightly sensed that the salaries appendage might find the public at large in an antagonistic mood. This proved only too true almost instantaneously. Garfield, for example, shortly discovered himself defensively driven to explaining his role and reasoning, both orally at community meetings and in a lengthy circular address for wide distribution among his constituents. The uproar brought results. By the time Congress reconvened the following December, 1873, it had become all too clear that the public would have none of the salaries escalation except that it be repealed. Almost immediately Congress undertook to rescind the legislation, only to discover that it had entrapped itself in two areas. Constitutionally, it could not undo its handiwork where federal judges and the president were concerned. Those salary increases necessarily continued in force.[14]

Nevertheless, the constitutional issue continued to rankle a clutch of congressmen through the next two years until they succeeded in revoking the increased salary. In

April 1874, Congressman Holman moved a pro forma amendment to the legislative, executive, and judicial appropriations bill for the pending fiscal year, seeking to reduce the president's salary to the original $25,000. Holman quoted the Constitution, arguing that its language on the point contained no troublesome ambiguity: "The President shall, at stated times, receive for his services a compensation, which shall neither be increased nor diminished during the period for which he shall have been elected . . . " Congress had acted unconstitutionally, according to Holman, when it raised the salary. It possessed "no more power" to do so on March 3, 1873, than at present. The words *term* and *period* were not identical, he insisted. Everyone could agree that the first meant four years. Not so the second word, which Holman thought had to be presumed to represent a careful, deliberate distinction. Consequently, Grant's "whole eight years together constituted the 'period' within the meaning of the clause . . . [and] the purpose of the Constitution was operating full force." For Holman, Congress had little choice but to "retrace its steps."[15]

Republican John A. Kasson of Iowa and Democrat Samuel S. Cox of New York lent their support. Kasson felt the founding fathers had intended to guarantee the partisan anonymity of the salary, by having it fixed "before the election had taken place and before they knew the man who was to be President." Cox, for his part, deplored the concentration of power in the hands of the federal government. In helping to decide this unusual question, he hoped to influence the government's aggrandizing tendency to focus "power and luxury" in the central bureaucracy. Americans wanted nothing as much as "frugal, simple and honest government," he believed, while the benefits accruing to the executive contributed to a contrary process.[16]

Republicans George F. Hoar and Henry L. Dawes, both of Massachusetts, were among those who were most troubled by the melding of salary and of services and expenses to where the differences had grown blurred and confusing. Hoar agreed that the original $25,000 no longer possessed its former value, but the services to and expenses provided by the government on behalf of the presidency too often projected "a very much larger sum than the salary which is fixed by law." Dawes, who had investigated the matter since the recent revision, urged a stricter definition between salary and expenses. It was no simple proposition, he discovered, to dispel the widespread impression that the president received emoluments additional to his salary of equal if not greater value.[17]

Republican Eugene Hale of Maine, who believed Holman's objection a largely "futile" argument, intervened to assure one and all that whatever the extravagances of government, the White House and its management did not figure among them. Since the "earliest days of our history" government had provided the president with the executive mansion and its furnishings, operations, maintenance, and office expenses. The whole represented public property temporarily placed at the president's disposal, which devolved to his successor upon his leaving the office. "Individual or family expenses," Hale explained, sharing his vantage from the Appropriations Committee, had never been the government's responsibility.[18]

Butler of Massachusetts, the bill's sponsor, stoutly seconded Hale's point, adding that many people had acquired the mistaken impression that the president realized personal advantages and benefits approaching $400,000 beyond the stated salary. Of course, this was wholly unfounded; in actual fact, several other officials were assisted by larger staffs than was the president. Relatively speaking, said Butler, the government expended less on White House operations than previously, when the total frequently included livery and equippage. These were now typically the president's property, part of his personal estate. The East Room ceiling collapsed some few years ago, Hale observed, dropping possibly a ton of plaster to the floor. Did the members seriously expect the president, Hale wondered, to see to the necessary repairs and restoration? Surely the nation deserved better than that the executive mansion should deteriorate to where it could hardly be distinguished from among scores of drab administrative bureaus.[19]

The amendment failed easily, much to the chagrin of those whose antagonisms had not been mollified. Although premature, their next attempt to lower the president's salary occurred within the year when two congressmen submitted legislation to that end in December 1874, during the last session of the Republican-dominated Forty-third Congress. At least one citizens' lobby, in support, forwarded a petition demanding the reversion of the salary to its traditional sum. The better timed of these efforts came in early 1876, in anticipation of the November general elections, and calculated to take effect on March 4, 1877. Senator George G. Wright, a Republican from Iowa, the instigator of the measure, reported the bill with the unanimous consent of the Committee on Civil Service and Retrenchment. To dramatize again that the president himself had been the beneficiary of the celebrated salary grab must have been among the most obvious of the several likely motives involved.[20]

Surprisingly, Wright's bill passed by six votes after only a modicum of debate. Fully twenty-seven members were absent during the brief interval, some of whom objected upon their return to the glaring haste that seemed to lay behind the successful manuever. Senator Sargent, the one member on hand to speak against the bill, labeled it "ineffable meanness" to cut the presidential salary to a figure below that which England paid its highest diplomatic representative in the United States. He persisted, even though the Senate moved on to other business, wondering at the penchant that impelled everyone to strive for the lowest possible salary levels generally and to single out the president in particular. The president, Sargent noted, received but an eighth of that paid his French counterpart and one half that provided the British diplomatic minister. The purpose, he concluded, seemed to be to cripple, perhaps "to destroy the public service." With a colleague's support, Sargent suggested a reconsideration of the hurried action.[21]

At this, Massachusetts's newly elected junior senator Henry L. Dawes, a Republican, reminded the floor of the "most unfortunate and unwise and pernicious" measure reponsible for the entire controversy, the act of 1873. The nation at large had made known its unmistakable opposition, so that it ill-behooved the Senate to preserve any vestige of it. Actually, he continued, higher salaries had never guaranteed greater purity in the public service. Comparative allusions to others' salaries in Europe served no useful purpose when the Prince of Wales received handsome revenues at the expense of "poor" and "starving" operatives manning England's dingy industrial mills.[22]

Senator George F. Edmunds, a Vermont Republican, indicated his displeasure at the parliamentary scheme employed during his brief absence from the floor. He noted how little evidence existed of the public's opposition to increasing the presidential salary, either in 1873 or at present. The furor had applied to the back-pay feature by which Congress had garnered a retroactive bonus for itself. Consequently, said Edmunds, Congress could not but admit its miscalculation. Americans, he believed, were "not a mean people," and desired the president be paid a sum adequate to maintaining the dignity of the office and suitable to conducting the business pertinent to it.[23]

Republican senator Timothy O. Howe of Wisconsin agreed. The $25,000 originally granted the president had not been for salary alone, which clearly would have been extravagant by any contemporary standard. The salary also represented a compensation for amenities the office required in order to "administer something like hospitality" in the name of the country as a whole. Otherwise it made little sense to provide the president with "a very large house to live in" and expenses beyond. It could hardly be doubted, Howe added, that the growth of the United States, both in population and wealth, had not produced an excess in the "grace of generosity" toward the president.[24]

Roscoe Conkling, New York's eccentric Republican senator, found the logic faulty. Recalling his opposition to every salary increase advanced since his election in 1859, a disingenous consistency now dictated his course. The public's reaction had been noted, he said; it had only to be obeyed. The question related neither to financial economy nor official merit. Rather, it dealt with the integrity of the popular will and the Senate's sworn duty to respect it. The *New York Times,* in a congenial mood, also detected no partisanship or disrespect toward the president. This latest endorsement of "simpler manners," therefore, seemed "likely to command the approval of the country."[25]

The motion to reconsider eventually failed, and the bill as adopted went over to the Democratic controlled

House in the divided Forty-fourth Congress. There it was referred to the Committee on Appropriations, which overnight gave it a favorable report. It passed without debate and by voice vote on April 6, 1876. Congressman Holman's tactics blocked a budding effort to move its reconsideration.[26]

Grant now found himself in the unique position of having to decide whether or not to slash his successor's salary to half the amount he received. He vetoed the reduction almost two weeks later in a bluntly worded, sometimes pointedly stated rejection of an affront to the "dignity of the position of Chief Magistrate" of the United States. In justification, Grant cited his personal experience with living costs at the White House and in the capital, his "duty" to the integrity of the presidency, and his belief that the citizenry wished a "fair compensation" paid their chosen officials commensurate with "our republican ideals and institutions." He wondered openly if there was not some motive to render the presidency an office "entirely of honor, when the salary should be abolished." Originally, he noted, congressional salaries had been but one-thirtieth of the president's. However, interim increases had elevated them to within one-fifth of it, even as the president's salary had lost four-fifths of its former value before meriting an adjustment. Its recent doubling, Grant implied, still left it proportionately deficient by about one-fifth, or $10,000.[27]

Grant's veto, upon its being returned to the Senate, was referred to the Committee on Retrenchment at the request of its chairman. Predictably, the committee recommended the chamber vote to override the action. The opportunity never arose; the leadership never brought the motion to the floor.[28]

The *New York Times,* in an editorial approving of

Grant's course of action, blamed "a combination of dem-agogues" and "a remnant of salary-grabbers" rather than finding any discernable party division. The one group had expected "to win some cheap applause," the other to man-age "a mean revenge" for its self-inflicted punishment on the excessive measure of 1873. Grant had proceeded cor-rectly and honorably, according to the *Times,* given the embarrassing trap that had been laid for him. The pres-ident needed the raise, the country could afford it, and the $50,000 at last placed him on a salary par with the governor of the Dominion of Canada. Congress had seen to nearly 600 percent in raises for itself since 1789, whereas the president's salary had been increased by a paltry 100 percent during the same period.[29]

In an earlier commentary, *The Nation* had attempted to plumb the history and logic of government salary schedules, discovering a fallacious mischief at work throughout. The operating assumption seemed to be that cheaper meant better, it announced, particularly when long lines of prospective applicants regularly haunted the government's central hiring offices. The entire condition could be attributed to the basically agrarian nature of the national economy. Those whose salaries were mea-sured by any gauge other than actual production, it explained, necessarily suffered. Public servants easily numbered among the most conspicuous of the lot.[30]

Some intransigents refused to yield. The approaching end of the presidential terms in 1879 and 1884 witnessed further attempts to return to the old order, before divided congresses in both instances. Although neither bill emerged from its assigned committee, press accounts typ-ically depicted retiring presidents as having profited by their tenure. Scotching one such report, ex-President R. B. Hayes belatedly revealed that he had departed the capital in 1881 with "less than a thousand dollars" in hand, nowhere near the $20,000 attributed to his estate.[31] A North Carolina congressman introduced still another retrenchment bill in 1892, seeking to cut the president's salary and a variety of other government expenses. Not until 1902 would there again be a bill, submitted by the nonvoting delegate from the Territory of Hawaii, to raise the salary.[32]

1. *Congressional Globe,* 34th Cong., 3d Sess., 1856–57, 1072, 1119.

2. Ibid., 32d Cong., 2d Sess., 1853, 903, 1139, and 1157.

3. Ibid., 42d Cong., 3d Sess., 1872–73, Pt. 1, 415–16, 607–08.

4. Ibid., Pt. 3, 1671–72; Howard P. Nash, Jr., *Stormy Petrel: The Life and Times of General Benjamin F. Butler, 1818–1893* (Rutherford: Fairleigh Dickinson University Press, 1969), 268.

5. *The Nation,* Vol. 6 (June 25, 1868), 508–09; ibid., Vol. 8 (March 4, 1869), 167–68.

6. Harry J. Brown and Frederick D. Williams, eds., *The Diary of James A. Garfield* (Michigan State University Press, 1967), Vol. 2, 156–57; Allan Peskin, *Garfield* (Kent State University Press, 1978), 366.

7. Brown and Williams, eds., *Diary of Garfield,* Vol. 2, 165; William B. Hesseltine, *Ulysses S. Grant* (New York: Frederick Ungar Publishing Co., 1957), 313–14.

8. *Congressional Globe,* 42d Cong., 3d Sess., 1872–73, Pt. 3, 1672–74.

9. Ibid., Pt. 3, 1674–78, 1904.

10. Ibid., Pt. 3, 2101.

11. Ibid., Pt. 3, 2104–05.

12. Ibid., Pt. 3, 2044–46.

13. Ibid., Pt. 3, 2046–51, 2182–84.

14. Brown and Williams, eds., *Diary of Garfield,* Vol. 2, 165.

15. U.S., *Congressional Record,* 43d Cong., 1st Sess., 1874, Pt. 4, 3124–25.

16. Ibid., Pt. 4, 3126, 3128.

17. Ibid., Pt. 4, 3125, 3127.

18. Ibid., Pt. 4, 3125.

19. Ibid., Pt. 4, 3125–26.

20. *New York Times,* 9, 14 December 1874, pp. 3 and 4, respectively; *Congressional Record,* 44th Cong., 1st Sess., 1876, Pt. 2, 1329.

21. *Congressional Record,* 44th Cong., 1st Sess., 1876, Pt. 2, 1696.

22. Ibid., Pt. 2, 1697.

23. Ibid.

24. Ibid., Pt. 2, 1698.

25. Ibid., Pt. 2, 1697; *New York Times,* 15 March 1876, p. 4.

26. *Congressional Record,* 44th Cong., 1st Sess., 1876, Pt. 2, 2267.

27. James D. Richardson, ed., *A Compilation of the Messages and Papers of the Presidents, 1789–1897* (Washington; GPO, 1899), Vol. 7, 380.

28. Hesseltine, *Grant,* 394; John A. Carpenter, *Ulysses S. Grant* (New York: Twayne Publishers, 1970), 128–29; *Congressional Record,* 44th Cong., 1st Sess., 1876, Pt. 3, 2577, 3311.

29. *New York Times,* 20 April 1876, p. 4.

30. *The Nation* 17 (February 23, 1873), 108–9.

31. *Congressional Record,* 46th Cong., 1st Sess., 1879, Pt. 2, 1728; ibid., 48th Cong., 1st Sess., 1883–84, Pt. 1, 290; Charles R. Williams, ed., *Diary and Letters of Rutherford B. Hayes* (Columbus: Ohio State Historical Society, 1925), Vol. 4, 640–41.

32. *Congressional Record,* 52d Cong., 1st Sess., 1891–92, Pt. 1, 729; ibid., 57th Cong., 1st Sess., 1902, Pt. 2, 1313.

3
Roosevelt

Theodore Roosevelt rarely eluded controversy for very long. It followed him almost everywhere, sometimes accidentally and scurrilously, at other times deliberately and beneficially. An instance of the undeserved variety occurred during the presidential campaign of 1904. Critics, chiefly the Democratic opposition, portrayed the president as guilty of vain and "snobbish extravagance" with public funds. They attacked him for attaching gilded stables to the White House, for appropriating a naval yacht to his family's selfish pleasure and appointing it with regal furnishings, and for laying down a park full of tennis courts on the executive grounds. All of it represented a blatant exaggeration, of course, and his supporters rightly blunted the accusations at every creditable turn.[1]

An instance of Roosevelt's ability to generate wholesome, often salient discussion began a year later, in September 1905. The president and his large young family had resided at the White House since 1901, save for part of 1902 when the century-old structure underwent extensive renovation and modernization costing nearly $500,000. Inaugurated to a full term the previous March 1905, Roosevelt, who had traveled more widely and entertained more frequently while in office than any predecessor, was a month short of his forty-seventh birthday, and a paragon of the strenuous life he yet popularized. All these elements now combined to produce an astonishing disclosure in the cause of executive leadership and initiative. The ensuing controversy would redound mostly in his favor, as Roosevelt confidently expected.[2]

In 1905, neither the president's salary, expenses, emoluments, nor perquisites encompassed a travel allowance. Presidents traditionally traveled little, and when they did, it was at their own or another's expense, usually the latter. At the time, most Americans were seemingly unaware that for at least a generation, the cost of transporting a traveling president had been absorbed directly by one or more railroads. Other favors, variously accepted or refused in an age less troubled by questions assuming conflict of interest, included personal insurance policies and, when necessary, hotel fees. The transportation gratuity had commenced under Abraham Lincoln, according to a presumably authoritative article that afterward appeared in *The Outlook,* when Roosevelt served on the editorial staff.[3] President Grover Cleveland may have been an exception to the rule, paying his own fare from profits realized through wise investments, but he too accepted the "courtesy of free transportation" for his secretary and aides. If the transportation eventually also meant a special private car, it indicated merely that experience had demonstrated a practical need beside the preservation of dignity. To transport the president during any regularly scheduled service only resulted in jumbled timetables, delayed connections, and inconvenienced passengers. Nor had it yet occurred to anyone that a presidential Pullman might well belong among the perquisites of the office.[4]

But as president, Roosevelt was different, as nearly everyone already knew, and he confessed "a horror of trying to save any money out of his pay." First, through his private secretary, he notified a railroad executive to prepare a special train and detailed itinerary for himself and several guests planning an extended tour across a bloc of states. Then, when the company hesitated because of the unavailability of certain requested equipment and suggested a "nominal" charge of fifty dollars per day, Roosevelt had his secretary lodge a telephone protest. Cordially, the railroad cooperated to the best of its ability. Roosevelt, however, also leaked the story to the press, emphasizing the utter absence of an authorized travel allowance and his dependence on public transportation. The press disseminated the story at just the moment when the issues of corporate lobbying, special rates, rebates, and free passes to the favored and powerful ranked high among a worried public's preoccupations with privilege and influence in a democratic society.[5]

Press reactions seem to have been friendly, despite Roosevelt's alleged "impropriety." A total of six bills had been introduced in Congress over the two sessions between 1904 and 1906 seeking to raise the president's and other officials' salaries. None of them ever emerged from its assigned committee. The case against the "shabby" and "parsimonious" compensations paid the nation's governing authorities, intermittently reactivated since the turn of the century, was gaining momentum, nevertheless.[6] By 1906, when the New York *Sun* publicly called for an appropriation to purchase an official train for the president's institutional use, the contrast between many "lucrative" private and most "meager" government salaries had been widely noted. In fact, Congress had already moved to increase its own stipends amid a consensus that for the first time expressly denied the benefit to those actually responsible for the legislation.[7]

Roosevelt's stratagem accomplished at least some of

the desired objectives. On June 20, 1906, the House Committee on Appropriations favorably reported a bill to authorize the president an optional fund of $25,000 to meet his travel expenses. It specifically replaced an earlier amendment to the sundry civil appropriations bill, which had been successfully protested on a point of order as constituting new legislation under House operating rules. The *New York Times,* among others, editorially cheered that the days of "Jeffersonian simplicity" were numbered, and remonstrated that the president was entitled to the same "decent and dignified" amenities as Congress. The issue involved less partisanship, observed the *Times,* than a shortsighted penury that belied the nation's wealth and rank. Details of the White House and executive housekeeping budgets had become better known as the press community examined and explained the controversy.[8]

On his part, Roosevelt took the next logical, if extraordinary step. He called a press conference on June 11, practically demanding the restoration of the travel budget to the legislative calendar. The fund would not redound to his personal advantage, he promised, but rather go to facilitate the legitimate business of the presidency. The nation's chief executive should not have to "travel as a dead head," Roosevelt explained, casting his language in railroad slang, nor in a style that, returning to formal usage, "violated every decent feeling of respect for this office."[9]

Again the press agreed. The *New York Times,* for example, thought Roosevelt's comments "unselfish, patriotic, and convincing." The national interest required passage of the bill on behalf of the "sole representative of all the people." A reluctant, Republican-controlled Fifty-ninth Congress listened. Cries for an investigation of the supposed "impropriety" eased. Hardly ten days later the House approved the separate measure by 176-68, although with 125 abstentions. The Senate followed suit the next day by a 42-20 margin. At last the president had recourse to a discretionary travel budget, which the energetic Roosevelt began to tap almost immediately.[10]

The debate, however, had been passionate, leaving in its aftermath some hard feelings destined to recur again. The objection in both chambers centered on the doubtful constitutionality of the proposal. The special fund, it was argued, amounted to an emolument explicitly prohibited by Article II of the Constitution, particularly if intended to benefit the incumbent. The costs of running the White House had grown by $70,000 since the presidency of William McKinley, noted Democratic congressman Oscar W. Underwood of Alabama, much of it directly advantageous to the first family. Yet, he continued, none of the president's offical duties "required him to travel about," no matter how receptive the public or better informed for it the president's views. According to Underwood, such travel could be justified only in the event of war or when the president assumed the role of commander-in-chief.[11]

Roosevelt himself obliquely conceded some of the theoretical merits of the argument. Midway through the proceedings he wrote the chairman of the House Committee on Appropriations, suggesting a likely compromise. Roosevelt proposed amending the bill to prevent the president's having personal access to the envisioned fund. Instead, he recommended restricting it to the purpose of enabling him to pay others' expenses—the president's staff and those journalists, officials, and "occasional private citizens" who were instructed or invited to accompany him. "Personally," Roosevelt said, "I should always rather travel on horseback than on a special train," not unlike some of the founding fathers. But, obviously, he noted dryly, the size of both the president's retinue and the nation had grown in the intervening century.[12]

As it developed, the bill became law without the need to advertise Roosevelt's compromise plan, and in an atmosphere which many felt permeated with suspense. The *New York Times* confessed its amazement at the Democratic partisanship associated with this "worthy" idea. The critics' "cheeseparing" attitude suggested a "mean frame of mind," it commented, ill-becoming both to Congress and the public interest when there was much to recommend moving beyond to consider as well the timeliness of acquiring a presidential train. The *Times,* again among others, endorsed the arguments of Congressman Bourke Cockran of New York. According to Cockran, "the Constitution can protect itself," as it always had; the presidency, alone among the main branches of government, ought not to be imprisoned in the late eighteenth century.[13]

The latent significance perceived in 1906 shortly surfaced in a comprehensive reappraisal of official salaries, notably the president's, especially in relation to other heads of state. First came a motion to pension retiring presidents at $25,000 a year as honorary members of the Senate. More bills to increase the president's basic salary followed. Meantime, the recently established travel allowance reappeared for its prescribed annual renewal. All three questions, singly and together, concentrated attention such as it had not been known since the days of Washington. Most of the attention, moreover, identified with the president's circumstances, until by 1909 a detectable reserve of good will had been collected in favor of taking some memorable and permanent action. Ex-President Grover Cleveland cast an early, open ballot for a "definite and generous provision . . . adequate to the situation," by which he seemingly meant a fixed pension requiring neither accountability nor obligations. An "easygoing thoughtlessness," he wrote six months before his death, better explained the tendency of republics than ingratitude. Some might regard former presidents as "relics," Cleveland elaborated, but most Americans typically desired to "continue them in service so far as to interfere seriously with their untrammeled return to private citizenship and their unrestrained resumption of the occupations of everyday life."[14]

On December 18, 1908, Republican senator Jonathan Bourne, Jr., of Oregon, introduced a bill to double the president's salary to $100,000 and the vice president's to $25,000, effective with the inauguration of the new administration on March 3, 1909. The *New York Times* editorially volunteered its support the next day, saying that the suggested increase was "moderate" given the many changed circumstances since the last revision, including the accumulation of national wealth. It expected the bill to "encounter no serious opposition."[15] The prediction proved correct in spirit, but wrong as to trajectory. Even allowing for the probable procedural difficulties and challenges, the ensuing debate comprised the single longest, most inclusive airing to attend the question after the original debate and settlement of 1789.

The routine legislative, executive, and judicial appropriations bill that passed the Republican-controlled House of the Sixtieth Congress at the turn of the year 1909 originally contained no entry relating to the presi-dent's salary. Senator Nelson A. Aldrich of Rhode Island, chairman of the Senate Finance Committee, attached the essense of Bourne's bill when the committee reported it favorably on January 8. The specifications sought to increase the salary to $100,000 upon condition of eliminating the recently established $25,000 travel allowance. Again the *Times* rushed an editorial reaction, claiming that the motion smacked of a "picayune proceeding" derogatory to a national government. The country was four times what it had been in Washington's day; thus, because the presidency meant at least four times the responsibilities, the salary should naturally reflect it. As for the travel allowance, said the *Times,* it was "neither graceful nor expedient" to withdraw what clearly belonged in the White House operating fund, not to mention the dubious principle at work in denying the allowance just three years after its creation.[16]

"Unexpected opposition" had visibly solidified on two fronts within ten days, excluding the rumored resistance being organized in the House. The Senate Committee on Appropriations tallied the president's perquisites and expenses to show that a "quite sufficient" total of $381,000 devolved in both general and incidental support, while others observed that the cost of the proposed salary increases for the nation's foremost elected officials exceeded $400,000. Meantime, Republican senator William E. Borah of Idaho led the fight to separate the measure on a point-of-order allegedly sustained by the Senate's rules manual. Eventually Borah's not inconsiderable parliamentary skills failed to win majority backing, but not before other, individualized reservations had exacted their toll, and a compromise began to appear necessary.[17]

Georgia's Democratic senator Alexander S. Clay refused to condone "sumptuous living" at public expense. He confessed himself prepared to argue for an enormous salary, possibly $200,000, he said, provided all the accumulated amenities and gratuities were discarded. Of course, said Clay, the dignity of the office had to be upheld, but experience had long shown that the "simple life, plain living and high thinking bring the best results." Senator Joseph W. Bailey, a Democrat from Texas, another advocate of "republican simplicity," concurred, with Vice President Charles W. Fairbanks presiding. "The President . . . lives a good deal like a piece of bric-a-brac," Bailey expatiated at some length, and the vice president had only "to sit in his place and do nothing." All those elected to the executive branch during the past twenty years, he believed, left their positions richer than when they entered them. An "embarrassed" Fairbanks capitulated, so to speak, when he shortly declined to rule on a troublesome point of order. The vice president called instead for a members' vote to resolve the procedural dispute.[18]

By now the *New York Times's* initial optimism had been shaken to where it acknowledged the delay. A salary of $100,000, it allowed, lay "beyond the range of experience" of most people, but were the issue put to a popular referendum, the *Times* had no doubt that "the native good sense and the self-respect of the people" would approve it. The character of the office not only justified the increase, it claimed, but even at the proposed amount, the salary still did not correspond to those received by other heads of state.[19]

Here proponents organized their forces and marshalled their comparisons and tabulations adequate to winning a partial, interim victory before returning the bill to the House. The central theme, elaborated by Bourne and ably extended by Republican senators Chauncey Depew of New York and Francis E. Warren of Wyoming, was this: Among the world's contemporary heads of state, the American president received a miniscule, "utterly ridiculous" fraction of the nation's total estimated wealth.

He received 1/1415th of 1 percent of all federal revenues, when his salary should be no less than 1/1200th, according to Bourne, whose folio of prepared tables and lists studiously documented the contention. Earlier presidents, he added, particularly those elected since James Buchanan in 1856, had none of them been wealthy men by any standard, and averaged five years of life beyond their terms. Republics were indeed ungrateful, to Bourne's mind, in two respects: They demanded that "the citizen should be first of all a patriot and then a Spartan." The precept counted for dogma, Bourne concluded, once a citizen attained the presidency.[20]

Both the press and public were impressed. The costs of maintaining the presidency, which one capital correspondent independently computed at $230,000 annually, were admittedly sizable. Yet Senator Bailey's alarm at the "tendency toward extravagance" seemed exaggerated as against the fact that the kings of England and Italy each received three million dollars per year, the Kaiser of Germany and the Emperor of Austria-Hungary four million dollars, and the Tsar of Russia something less than the twelve million dollars divulged a few years past. Purists emphasized that even the president of the kindred Republic of France was paid the equivalent of $125,000. And a New York City woman voluntarily contributed an omission: The president of the impoverished island-country of Haiti received $35,000, only $15,000 less than his American counterpart.[21]

Finally on January 19, in what the *New York Times* called a "spectacular contest," the Senate narrowly voted 35-30 to fix the president's salary at $100,000, although minus the travel allowance annually renewed since 1906. A motion to split the difference at $75,000 fared better than did the idea of keeping the salary at its former level.

A last-minute push to arrange for a yearly reconsideration of the settled amount also failed, as did Senator Borah's subsequent effort to force a reconsideration on procedural objections. The increase had been achieved partly at the expense of the speaker of the House and the vice president, both of whose salaries were raised by a diminished $3,000 each, from $12,000 to $15,000. The president's cause had been hurt by Roosevelt's having spent for the fiscal year only $9,000 of his travel budget, but helped by the knowledge that the president-elect was a person of moderate means.[22]

Already, however, reports circulated of House disappointment with the smallness of the speaker's salary raise. In fact, the House and Senate conference committee spent the whole of February trying, without success, to reconcile the many vexing differences between the two versions of the bill. Although the House early showed a disposition to add to the perquisites of the presidency, including an authorization of $12,000 with which to purchase some of the first White House automobiles, there was much reluctance to revising the president's salary. A deadlock developed by February 10. House Democrats resurrected their dormant constitutional objections to the perpetuation of the travel allowance, still insisting that it represented a prohibited emolument. Conversely, so-called Republican "insurgents" in the Senate demurred at so grand a sum as $100,000.[23]

Others in both chambers pointed to the strained federal budget and looming deficit as good and sufficient reasons to resist a variety of salary adjustments totaling in excess of $300,000. Republican congressman James Mann from Illinois acknowledged the president's personal popularity, but remained convinced that "every President, no matter what is his salary, spends it as fast as he gets it." Democrats Champ Clark of Missouri and Gilbert M. Hitchcock of Nebraska deplored the comparisons to foreign heads of state, particularly the royal houses of Europe. "The House owes it to this country as a duty," said Hitchcock, "to put its stamp of disapproval promptly upon this effort to create practically regal conditions in the White House, imitating ceremony, imitating the extravagance, imitating the luxury of the courts of the Old World." Kentucky Democrat A. O. Stanley applauded the difference that sprang "from the inherent and eternal variance between the genius of a republic and a monarchy." "Our Presidents," he continued, "have exercised their authority while living the simple life of a citizen, his children attending the common schools, neither seeking nor receiving crowns and coronets . . . his home modest, almost devoid of equipage and luxury, pretension or display." Above all, "these Presidents have surrendered their mighty commissions without effort or regret, returning to the people and resuming without loss of dignity the duties of a citizen."[24]

Proponents of the measure, notably Democrat Cockran of New York, Roosevelt's personal friend, commended the president for his "ideal life . . . so far as expenditures are concerned," which he pronounced free of both extravagance and ostentation. In fact, Cockran observed, most if not all the presidents, at least since Grant's time, had clung to the same sense of decorum. The $50,000 salary, which enabled them to accomplish it, now required an upward adjustment. Cockran thought it curious that the House, possibly the highest paid legislative body in the world, had always been keen to hold down everyone's salary but its own. "No president can live on less than the full amount . . . now paid him," Cockran advised, "if he continues to occupy the dwelling provided for him."

Moreover, it was inconsistent to equate the president's salary with institutional perquisites when Congress had seen to many of the same privileges for itself. Congressman William Sulzer, also a New York Democrat, offered his support. He had been surprised in 1906 at the volume of favorable mail and editorial agreement after submitting a bill to revise the salary.[25]

But the most common and convincing theme developed dealt with the postpresidential careers of former presidents. There was a broad sympathetic concern that ex-presidents represented a special problem to themselves and for the country as a whole. To be sure, few doubted that a regular pension would find the public recalcitrant. Yet, many also agreed that little if any of the salary could be saved against a president's return to civilian life. Cockran thought it particularly instructive that after losing the election of 1888, Cleveland took employment in a large law partnership in New York City, where he was retained as a counselor, among others, to a leading insurance company. While the president was "engaged in our service," Cockran maintained, "we should afford him such compensation that, by the exercise of reasonable economy, he can choose his own method of life after leaving office." Democratic congressman Richard P. Hobson of Alabama concurred, believing that no one seriously wished to witness retired presidents "driven to enter competitive pursuits to keep the wolf from the door." The country possessed the pride and wealth to afford better, he contended.[26]

These and allied arguments contained a powerful impetus for revising the salary so that future presidents might be spared from "sinking into distress," if not wholly shielded from exposure to occupational "criticism and reproach." Thus, the adjustment consciously featured an informal, built-in concession to a retirement fund. The House in the end defeated the Senate's $100,000 salary proposal on February 24 by 168–141. It accepted a compromise motion of $75,000 plus continuation of the travel allowance by 163–149.[27]

The conferees met again on March 2, to no avail. The next day, as the adjournment deadline approached, stalemated negotiations continued. Executive salaries formed the vital stumbling block in the most important piece of legislation still outstanding. Should the bill not pass before noon on March 4, all salaries would remain as previously fixed. At last, late on March 3, the necessary compromises developed. The salaries of the vice president, speaker, and Supreme Court justices would stay the same. Only the president's salary would increase, to $75,000 annually minus the separate travel account. The Senate had yielded to House insistence on the lesser of the two sums proposed. Roosevelt approved the bill among the final acts of his presidency prior to the inauguration of William Howard Taft. It was no small victory for someone who repeatedly admitted an ignorance of economics and who willingly delegated to others management of his personal finances.[28]

Taft became a notable exception in the roster of American presidents. In combination, the raise, the nation's economic stability, and the restoration of the travel allowance after a brief hiatus made his tenure an unusually contented and rewarding one for him. In fact, Taft might have become the first president to enjoy a pension had he consented to an extraordinary proposal in 1912. Industrialist Andrew Carnegie, who clearly liked Cleveland's earlier suggestion, offered to provide retiring presidents or their widows with a grant of $25,000 annually until Congress saw fit to correct its negligence in this regard.

Taft rejected the generosity, ostensibly because of complaints against consigning past chief executives to a disparaging dependence upon a millionaire's dole.[29]

1. *The Outlook* 76 (April 1904), 868–70; Sylvia J. Morris, *Edith Kermit Roosevelt: Portrait of a First Lady* (New York: Coward, McCann, and Geoghgan, 1980), 277.

2. William Ryan and Desmond Guinness, *The White House: An Architectural History* (New York: McGraw-Hill, 1980), 151–52; Morris, *Roosevelt,* 199, 264–65, who noted that Mrs. Roosevelt opposed her husband's acceeding to the vice presidency partly because it meant $2,000 less in salary than the governorship of New York and no publicly supported domicile. Here I borrow the viewpoint employed by Willard B. Gatewood, Jr., *Theodore Roosevelt and the Art of Controversy* (Baton Rouge: Louisiana State University Press, 1970).

3. Abridged and quoted in the *New York Times,* 21 January 1911, 5; Edward S. Corwin, *The President: Office and Powers, 1787–1957* (New York: New York University Press, 1957), 349.

4. *New York Times,* 24 May 1905, p. 1.

5. Roosevelt quoted in Morris, *Roosevelt,* pp. 264–65; *Literary Digest,* Vol. 31 (October 14, 1905), 521–22.

6. *Literary Digest,* Vol. 32 (June 23, 1906), 930–31; *Congressional Record,* 58th Cong., 3d Sess., 1904–05, Pt. 1, 123, 544, and 616; Adelbert H. Steele, "Shabby Salaries of Our Public Officials," *Gunton's Magazine* 18 (May 1900), 419–28; Thomas L. James, "The United States a Parsimonious Employer," *North American Review* 182 (February 1906), 266–74.

7. Katherine E. Thomas, "How a President Spends His Salary," *New England Magazine* 33 (1905–06), 272–76; Hubert E. Fuller, "Congressional Salary Legislation," *North American Review* 188 (October 1908), 539–51.

8. *New York Times,* 11 June 1906, 6; *World's Work* 12 (May 1906), 7482–83.

9. *New York Times,* 12 June 1906, 1.

10. Ibid., 13 June 1906, 8; ibid., 22 June 1906, 7; ibid., 23 June 1906, 6.

11. *Congressional Record,* 59th Cong., 1st Sess., 1906, pt. 9, 8809–11.

12. Roosevelt to James A. Tawney, June 17, 1906, in Elting E. Morison, ed., *Letters of Theodore Roosevelt* (Cambridge: Harvard University Press, 1952–55), Vol. 5, 303–04.

13. *Congressional Record,* 59th Cong., 1st Sess., 1906, pt. 9, 8811–12; *New York Times,* 23 June 1906, p. 6.

14. *New York Times,* 22 March 1908, 2, 2; ibid., 18 December 1908, 1; Grover Cleveland, "Our People and Their Ex-Presidents," *Youth's Companion 82,* (January 2, 1908), 3–4.

15. *New York Times Ibid., 19 December 1908, 8.*

16. *Ibid., 8 January 1909, 1; ibid., 9 January 1909, 6.*

17. *Congressional Record,* 60th Cong., 2d Sess., 1908–9, Pt. 1, 930–50; *New York Times,* 13, 16 January 1909, 1 and 4, respectively.

18. *Congressional Record,* 60th Cong., 2d Sess., 1908–9, Pt. 1, 940, 1035–37; *New York Times,* 17, 19 January 1909, 10 and 2, respectively.

19. *New York Times,* 17 January 1909, 10.

20. *Congressional Record,* 60th Cong., 2d Sess., 1908–9, pt. 2, 1025–33.

21. *Literary Digest* 38 (January 30, 1909), 162–64; *The Independent* 66 (February 18, 1909), 341–42; *New York Times,* 19 January 1909, 8.

22. *Congressional Record,* 60th Cong., 2d Sess., 1908–9, Pt. 2, 1096, 1293–94; *New York Times,* 20, 23 January 1909, 1 and 2, respectively.

23. *New York Times,* 2 February 1909, 2; ibid., 6 February 1909, 1; ibid., 25 February 1909, 2.

24. *Congressional Record,* 60th Cong., 2d Sess., 1908–09, Pt. 4, 3026–30.

25. Ibid., Pt. 4, 3030–32; James McGurrin, *Bourke Cockran: A Free Lance in American Politics* (New York: Scribner's Sons, 1948), pp. 279–80, 284–85.

26. *Congressional Record,* 60th Cong., 2d Sess., 1908–09, Pt. 4, 3032–33; Allan Nevins, *Grover Cleveland: A Study in Courage* (New York: Dodd, Mead & Co., 1932), p. 443.

27. *Congressional Record,* 60th Cong., 2d Sess., 1908–09, Pt. 4, 3033–34.

28. *New York Times,* 3 and 4 March 1909, 2 and 3, respectively; Edward Wagenknecht, *The Seven Worlds of Theodore Roosevelt* (New York: Longman, Green & Co., 1958), pp. 210–16.

29. *New York Times,* 28 April 1909, 1; John W. Chambers II, "Presidents Emeritus," *American Heritage* 30 (June–July, 1979), 18.

4
The Last Tax-exempt President

Early in the administration of William Howard Taft, the Republican-dominated Sixty-first Congress passed a proposed amendment to the Constitution, authorizing the imposition of a graduated income tax on personal incomes "from whatever source derived." By the end of 1912, thirty-four state legislatures had voted their assent to the measure. West Virginia joined the list during January 1913. Then three states—Delaware, Wyoming, and New Mexico—vied to complete the mandatory minimum of thirty-six. On February 25, the secretary of state presided over formalities in the capital certifying that the Sixteenth Amendment had been duly ratified, the first constitutional revision in forty-three years.[1] One week later Woodrow Wilson was inaugurated the twenty-eighth president of the United States.

The House of Representatives shortly began to fashion an income-tax policy designed to take retroactive effect on March 1. Adopted in October, the finished legislation required every adult citizen to submit annually a statement of gross income realized during the previous calendar year. Necessarily, however, the policy also accredited several practices inherited from past experience then believed to possess a constitutional sanction. These practices included the president's salary because of the terms contained in Article II pertaining to an imcumbent. Consequently, Congress specified that "in computing net income . . . there shall be excluded the compensation of the present President . . . during the term for which he shall have been elected, and of the judges of the supreme and inferior courts . . . now in office, and the compensation of all officers and employees of a State or any political subdivision thereof except when such compensation is paid by the United States government."[2]

The exclusion benefited both Taft and Wilson. Taft, whose administration had supported the amendment and whose presidency ended on March 4, 1913, observed the law. In completing the newly introduced Form 1040 in 1914, Taft marked his prorated salary of $625 for the final three days of his tenure as "exempted by the Constitution." Wilson, who had been elected Taft's successor in November 1912, simply left blank the appropriate entry for the nine-month salary he received in 1913.[3]

Edwin Seligman, a reigning expert on the history of taxation and sometime tax consultant and advisor, thought the provision fair and reasonable under the circumstances. These salaries, he wrote in the revised edition of his comprehensive survey completed in March 1914, "are exempt out of regard for the constitutional provision prohibiting any diminution of their compensation while in office."[4] This simple summation obscured the extent of a problem as yet imperfectly considered. Seligman accurately recognized that the Sixteenth Amendment challenged some precedents created during the past century. But he incorrectly assumed that the amendment superseded certain parts of Articles II and III of the Constitution, and like Congress itself, evidently believed that with the general elections of 1916, the presidential exemption would terminate forever. Not so. The stage had been set for a complicated constitutional drama that twenty years of litigation and regulatory interpretation did not finally resolve.

Prior to 1912, no president imagined that his prescribed salary might be liable to taxation. A national tax formed no part of the constitutional settlement in 1789; during the two occasions in the nineteenth century when Congress briefly instituted the tax, presidents were presumed exempted by constitutional fiat or ultimately confirmed in that status. The taxes the Confederate States of America assessed its president provided no relevant exception;[5] while a literal reading of Article II, Section 1, of the Constitution tended to wall off the entire topic outside the arena of open debate.

The same principle, replicated in Article III, insulated federal judges even more successfully. Associate Justice Samuel F. Miller of the Supreme Court, in an influential lecture series of 1889 marking the centennial of the Constitution, pronounced the rule "a wise one." It helped to insure the mutual independence of the three branches of government, said Miller, and to safeguard the Executive and Judiciary against Legislative encroachment.[6]

Indeed, the two most important precedents sustained Miller's view for just those reasons. The executive and judiciary, respectively, had earlier reversed actions taken by Congress during domestic crises. In the first instance, Presidents Abraham Lincoln and Andrew Johnson, unlike the justices of the Supreme Court,[7] paid voluntarily and without complaint the 3 and 5 percent levies that Congress reluctantly imposed on federal salaries in 1862 and 1864. However, in 1872 the Treasury Department, on the strength of an 1869 opinion from the attorney general holding an exemption constitutionally valid, issued refund warrants for the amounts withheld. Lincoln's family, for example, received a total of $3,555 deducted from the president's annual salary of $25,000.[8]

Not war but economic distress, the depression of 1893 prompted Congress's second enactment of an income tax. President Grover Cleveland evidently prepared the appropriate statement in 1895, only to have it nullified within the year by a narrow, controversial Supreme Court ruling that invalidated all direct taxation under federal aegis except as apportioned among the states according to population. Senior staff at the Bureau of Internal Revenue afterward described Cleveland's unquestioning declaration a report of "net annual income under the law."[9]

In 1913, the first session of the Democratic dominated Sixty-third Congress acknowledged these precedents when, uncertain of the scope of its new mandate, it showed little disposition "to raise any constitutional argument" not substantially related to the subject at hand. In excusing the incumbent president and presiding federal judges, Congress waved the "small amount" of taxes involved in the belief that it had limited the exemptions to a particular term of office or officer's tenure.[10] It intended that the exemption should cease starting in 1916, if not before, as for example upon a judge's retirement. As adopted, therefore, the tax code expressly relieved President Wilson from paying taxes on his salaried income through 1916, but not of his duty to file a tax return on his other private resources.

Wilson remembered the obligation shortly before the first anniversary of his inauguration. "What do I have to do and how do I have to do it?" he asked of his secretary of treasury in late February, 1914. Secretary William G.

McAdoo dispatched the proper form under a note advising the president that "as you are probably aware, the Income Tax Law specifically exempts your compensation." Wilson acted accordingly. His completed return for 1913 omitted any mention of his presidential salary of $75,000. His tax returns for 1914, 1915, and 1916 repeated the same procedure, including any shortened marginal justification such as Taft had entered. Wilson paid an income tax of less than $1,000 for each year of his first term, chiefly on earned interest on securities, stock dividends, and book royalties.[11]

The president's traditional tax exemption theoretically expired with the general elections of November 1916, no matter that Wilson had been reelected for a second term. The landmark Revenue Act of that year, sometimes called the War Preparedness Bill, featured a federal tax policy noticeably biased against concentrated wealth and privileged groups and inclined toward "equalitarianism."[12] The declaration of war voted the following April supplied a powerful, compelling impetus to the attitudinal shift inherent in the measure, which in turn strongly influenced the Emergency Revenue Act passed in October 1917, by the Democratically dominated Sixty-fourth Congress.

Except for the introductory phrasing, the language in both revenue measures exactly duplicated that which appeared in the Tax Bill of 1913, with one small, some might say clever, difference: "The following income shall be exempt from the provisions of this title: . . . the compensation of the present President . . . during the term for which he has been elected, and the judges of the Supreme and inferior courts . . . now in office, and the compensation of all officers and employees of a State, or any political subdivision thereof, except when such compensation is paid by the United States government."[13] The added punctuation, the insertion of a comma between "thereof" and "except" toward the close of the paragraph introduced a qualification, altering the meaning of the preceding whole. What at first appeared a statement of allowable exemptions ended, instead, by suggesting the opposite, ostensibly eliminating them for all the positions and categories named.

Congress had gingerly tested the vulnerability of all federal personnel to salary taxation, although so ambiguously that Joseph P. Tumulty, Wilson's private secretary, sought a legal clarification on behalf of the White House. The solicitor of the Bureau of Internal Revenue replied affirmatively; the president's compensation was fully taxable, according to the Revenue Acts of 1916 and 1917. Consequently, the solicitor noted, Wilson would need to revise the tax return recently filed for 1917. (There was no mention of any revision due on 1916 taxes.) Wilson, pleading too many demands on his time to attend to the matter personally, turned the task over to bureau staff, who proceeded to incorporate his salary for the ten months beginning with his second inauguration in March. As a result, Wilson paid an income tax of $6,800, nearly $6,000 more than in any previous year.[14]

The war-induced Revenue Act of 1917 injected an element of urgency into tax policy. In addition to raising tax rates dramatically, it treated all traditional exemptions skeptically and pitted the House leadership against the administration and Senate majority on the issue of excess profits versus war profits. Congressman Claude Kitchin, Democratic majority leader, adamantly favored an excess-profits tax to meet the extraordinary financial demands of World War I, while the administration argued for the adequacy of a war-profits schedule. Kitchin prevailed despite the weight of the opposition, eventually persuading the administration to endorse his recommendations.[15] The bill reached a joint conference committee in early October. At this point House conferees, following Kitchin's lead, insisted on a surprise amendment to Section 209 dealing with an excess-profits tax of 8 percent on annual salaries of $6,000 and higher. The amendment specified that "This title shall apply to all trades or businesses of whatever description, whether continuously carried on or not, except—(a)In the case of officers and employees under the United States or any State, Territory, or the District of Columbia, or any local subdivision thereof, the compensation or fees received by them as such officers and employees."[16]

Capital correspondents quickly sensed an unusual story. The newly inserted provision involved "a disturbing matter" to lawyers, engineers, physicians, and bank and corporate heads, who warily labeled the "joker" an undisguised species of double taxation. Internal Revenue spokesmen pleaded no prior knowledge or responsibility. On Wall Street, bond quotations plunged to a four-year low. New York City attorneys developing a specialty in tax law pondered its meaning and calculated its effects.[17]

Reduced to essentials, the provision seemed to spare congressmen and senators from the force of the excess-profits tax even as it singled out professional persons independently able to establish their fees. Reportedly, the provision, if adopted, would also relieve cabinet-level appointees, the speaker of the House, and the vice president each of $480 in income taxes, and ambassadors of $920. The president, however, would be liable to another $5,520.[18] Clearly, to define the difference between government employees and officers, both elected or appointed, admitted of no easy solution in matters of taxation. Subsequent efforts in later sessions to master these subtle distinctions also floundered in the same arcane complexities.

Congressman Kitchin of North Carolina, an intellectual disciple of William Jennings Bryan, and the contentious, antiwar and anticonscription chairman of the Ways and Means Committee, defended his brainchild after Senator Boies Penrose of Pennsylvania identified him as its author. Kitchin, said Penrose, had threatened to deadlock the conference committee if Senate representatives refused to accept the amendment. For his part, Kitchin frankly confessed it an exemption, declaring that "the government is not a business institution and no salary therefrom is a business income." "No government in the world (and I mean that)," he emphasized, "places an excess profits tax upon the salaries of its officials." Theirs was a compensation for service, not a remuneration. "Personally," Kitchin confided to the press, "I am in Congress at a loss."[19]

Republican senators Reed Smoot of Utah and James Wadsworth of New York vowed to kill the "joker." Congressman Cordell Hull of Tennessee, architect of the original tax code of 1913, said Kitchin might be technically correct, but blind to the "injustice of Congressmen exempting themselves from the general policy which they themselves establish." In Hull's view, Kitchin's provision had opened Congress "to a charge of self-favoritism" and, worse, impugned the government as a whole.[20]

The chairman's flanking maneuver failed. Kitchin offered not an explanation of his purpose, commented the *New York Times,* but an oblique confession "about as poor as could be devised." It was one thing to risk denunciation, quite another and "always more dangerous" to invite ridicule.[21]

By December, four bills had been introduced, deliberately aimed at defeating the "closed door" amendment. Republican congressman Nicholas Longworth of Ohio led the repeal fight in the Ways and Means Committee. He wished he could impute lofty motives to the proposal, he said, but even were it possible, the din of the public's "severe" reaction to it had deafened all hearing. The Bureau of Internal Revenue, inclined at first to accede to the amendment as another of the "various perquisites" of office, soon set about instructing Congress in the wholly unprecedented character of the exemption. Although Longworth's own repeal motion failed of adoption, that presented by retiring Congressman Charles H. Dillon of South Dakota succeeded. The House voted 308-1 to deny itself the novel dispensation, which meant individual tax obligations of at least $120 more for each member receiving the base salary of $7,500 per year.[22]

"Kitchinism" produced its ultimate expression in 1918 in yet another war revenue bill designed to raise eight billion dollars through taxation—or, as the chairman himself publicly explained, twice the amount ever attempted by any nation in a single year. Almost four-fifths of the total would be drawn from income, inheritance, and excess-profits taxes—on steeply graduated scales. A "perfectly equitable" tax law was not possible, Kitchin wrote, and everyone, including presumably the president, should willingly shoulder a share of the burden. *The Outlook* magazine, among others, readily agreed to the principle. "Taxation should reach as many, not as few, citizens as possible," it asserted. "We must not jeopardize our spirit of democracy.[23]

To this end, the bill expressly declared what had been strongly suggested earlier. Parenthetically attached to a general definition of those who comprised taxpayers, the bill proclaimed the cessation of all special exemptions except as provided for in the measure itself. The income tax, it announced, applied to all adult citizens without exception, including "the President of the United States, the judges of the Supreme Court and the inferior courts . . . and all other officers and employees, whether elected or appointed, of the United States" and its territories.[24]

The committee's accompanying report openly admitted that "the compensation of these officials under existing law is not subject to income tax." It plainly acknowledged the "great difference of opinion among the best legal talent" as to the constitutionality of the committee's contention. Nevertheless, the report concluded, "all equity and justice" required legislative approval and official compliance.[25]

A clutch of critics from both parties dwelt on the separation of powers, noted the utter absence of supporting precedents, cited at least two recent antagonistic Supreme Court decisions, and proposed two emasculating amendments. All to no avail. Kitchin and his committee of twenty-three were not to be denied. Congressman Henry T. Rainey of Illinois, averring that his constituency would tolerate no more talk of exemptions, even insinuated that the Constitution had become a refuge for "shirkers." For his part, Kitchin insisted on the universality of citizenship, both in its obligations as well as its rights. He prevailed by resorting to his ready wit and by demanding that Congress cease a futile debate and, instead, enable the courts to resolve the issue.[26]

"We cannot settle it; we have not the power to settle it," Kitchin argued on the House floor. "Let us raise it, as we have done, and let it be tested; and it can only be done by some one protesting the tax and taking an appeal to the Supreme Court." His colleagues concurred; no one called for a separate vote on the issue. The bill in its entirety passed some days later by an overwhelming margin. Wilson allegedly observed, perhaps too complacently, that once the "distinguished stubborn North Carolinian . . . made up his mind he would never open it."[27]

In the Senate, the Committee on Finance performed radical surgery on the bill over a long weekend, extracting or dissecting whole sections before releasing it to floor debate. The provisions to tax the president's and judges' salaries disappeared under the committee's scalpel. Senator Robert M. LaFollette of Wisconsin, leader of the objecting minority, failed in an attempt to restore it and a variety of other deleted provisions. However, again in conference committee, House spokesmen succeeded in having the clause reinstated, sacrificing some points on inheritance and estate taxes in order to accomplish it.[28]

Senator Charles H. Thomas of Colorado, a member of the Finance Committee, stood firm in his opposition to three "obnoxious" features in the compromise bill, including the attack on the presidential tax exemption. To impose the tax, he said, was to "ignore a plain constitutional inhibition and deprive those concerned of all remedy against the consequences." Never before had such a tax appeared in comparable legislation. In fact, he added, not altogether accurately, that the president's and judges' salaries had been "expressly excepted" in the Revenue Acts of 1913, 1916, and 1917. Nothing had changed in the interim to warrant the departure, regardless of the fulsome need generated by the war. Citing Alexander Hamilton in *The Federalist,* Thomas lectured his colleagues on the Constitution's care to insure the integrity of the executive and independence of the judiciary. "Both are at the mercy of the legislative branch from the hour that the power of taxing these salaries is conceded."[29]

Eventually the Senate, Thomas included, yielded once an impasse loomed over excess-profits and estate taxes. Hearings, delays, and repetitious wrangling had already postponed resolution of the Revenue Bill until the third, extended session of the Sixty-fifth Congress. Finally, in February, 1919, the House adopted its handiwork by a decisive majority, although with ninety-three abstentions. The Senate, spent and distracted, permitted a simple voice vote to suffice. "The idea of taking credit for the bill," the *New York Times* editorialized, "occurred to nobody." Wilson, lately returned from the peace conference in Paris, approved without comment the measure on February 24.[30]

Thomas's "unthinkable" prediction of the judiciary having "to sit in judgment of themselves" now came true. Walter Evans, judge for the Western District of Kentucky (Louisville) since 1899, filed suit for the tax collected on his $12,000 salary for 1918. The Southern District Court denied his contention, whereupon Judge Evans appealed the case to the Supreme Court. Justice Willis Van Devanter wrote the majority opinion handed down on June 1, 1920, nullifying the pertinent portion of the act when applied to presiding judges confirmed of appointment prior to its adoption. Van Devanter emphasized the provocative character of the legislation, pointedly citing Kitchin's public remarks and his committee's report, and found additional support in Wilson's published study of *Constitutional Government in the United States* (1908). Five years later, in Miles vs. Graham, the Supreme Court broadened the decision to protect all federal judges against the tax. Thereafter, until 1937, the judges remained largely exempt from the national income tax law.[31]

Curiously, the press and public took little interest in the issue or the contest it posed among the main branches of government. The *New York Times,* for example, merely reported the departure on exemptions early in the legislative proceedings, never developed an editorial on the theme, and printed only one citizen's letter deploring the constitutional challenge it presented. *The Nation's* analysis of the bill for an admittedly disinterested public ignored the exemptions issue. Ex-President Taft, who wrote an article for the *Ladies' Home Journal* in support of raising the presidential salary to $100,000, mentioned the matter not at all among numerous personalized instances of higher living costs, accrued White House customs, and often inescapable social and civic demands. An economist at the University of Minnesota noted the repeated ambiguity in Congress's declarations, but expected the courts in any case to respect the Constitution, at least to the extent of prohibiting attempted enforcement upon those elected to office before the law took effect. Prof. Edward S. Corwin of Princeton University, a close student of constitutional history, evidently spoke the prevailing sentiment. He recognized the "strict logic" by which the Court had arrived at its position, yet insisted it "furnishes no reason for building up a privileged class of property holders exempt from taxation by the national government as to their incomes."[32] Popular indifference, it seems likely, here passed for assent.

Did the president also intend to make a federal case of it? Wilson first considered his position in September 1918, while the Senate fitted the measure into its legislative calendar. According to Edward M. House, his intimate confidant and chief advisor, Wilson "had in mind contesting the tax" as an "infringement of the Constitution" possibly portending "serious results." He would pay the tax, if he must, to indicate the money was unimportant as compared to his collateral legal "action" in defense of the principle that Congress could neither punish nor reward the president through his salary. Colonel House successfully dissuaded him, reasoning that "it would not look well" for the president personally to prompt such a suit, that his "motives would certainly be misconstrued," and that others in the administration, namely Attorney General Thomas W. Gregory, could convey his objection presuming mitigation to political friends in the Senate.[33]

Gregory failed, whatever his efforts. Under retroactive provisions contained in the Revenue Act of 1918, Wilson's tax liabilities soared by $20,000, from less than $7,000 to almost $27,000 because of hefty surtax charges computed on an exaggerated scale that attained heights of 63 percent. Small wonder was that he had difficulty in raising the money, despite the special withholding arrangement of $125 per month initiated in March 1917, or that many errands and details fell to Wilson's brother-in-law, John R. Bolling, while the president himself readied for his return voyage to France and nearly four months more of deliberations at the Paris Peace Conference.[34]

Wilson's taxable income for 1919, the year he suffered a paralyzing, permanently enfeebling stroke, climbed by still another $1,500. At the collector's suggestion, Wilson took advantage of the prescribed installment plan, although it meant accumulating interest charges of one-half of one percent on the unpaid balance.[35] The initial payment of $7,080, a required one-fourth of the whole, had been forwarded when Judge Evans appealed his case to the Supreme Court. The White House must have been tracking its progress, for on March 6, 1920, barely one day after the Court heard oral arguments on the case, it filed two claims with the collector's office. One claim requested refund of the entire 1918 salary tax; the other requested abatement of the outstanding balance on the president's 1919 taxes, plus refund of all but $897 of the single installment previously paid, including the eighty-one dollar interest charge for tardiness. Both claims confidently cited the decision pending in Evans vs. Gore and implied that the president would abide by the Court's verdict.[36]

Wayne Johnson, Internal Revenue solicitor, believed the Revenue Act of 1918 unconstitutional as it concerned the presidential salary. An opinion had been sought of the attorney general, however, who took the opposite view. The bureau could not but proceed accordingly, said Johnson, although he fully expected a Court verdict before Wilson's second payment on installment fell due. Once the refund claims had been signed and returned, Johnson added, "I will see [that] they are filed in a confidential manner so that no publicity may attach to them."[37]

The Court's 7–2 decision in Evans vs. Gore, explained in one of the longer judgments "rendered in recent years," sustained the plaintiff and ordered his tax payments redeemed. Wilson entered his salary on the tax returns for 1920 and the applicable portion of 1921, through his departure from office in March, annotating the entry in both instances as being legally exempted from taxation.[38] The Bureau of Internal Revenue did not dispute it and honored the refund and abatement claims earlier submitted. Wilson's income taxes dropped to the modest amounts typical of his first term. Again the press took little notice of the finer points. So far as the *New York Times* was concerned, ex post facto constraints, not Evans vs. Gore, shielded the incumbent against the full force of income-tax legislation and its interpretation. The advantage would not survive him. Whomever the president elected in November 1920, the *Times* offhandedly and cryptically suggested, he would have no recourse but to comply with the law.[39]

Actually, President-elect Warren G. Harding might have chosen among three alternatives. He could invoke the precedent created by his predecessor, resting heavily on the untested corollary of Evans vs. Gore; he could initiate a separate suit in the name of the executive, seeking to have the Court confirm for it what it had secured the judiciary; or he could choose to pay income taxes after the manner of any private citizen. There were some inclined to facilitate Harding in reaching a decision. In early February 1921, Congressman Herbert C. Pell, Jr., of New York, a single term, lame-duck Democrat, introduced a bill in the Republican-controlled Sixty-sixth Congress specifically exempting the salaries of the president and vice president from the provisions of the national income tax law. Pell's motives are not immediately clear.[40]

The bill became superfluous within a matter of days. Congressman Longworth shortly wrote the president-elect on behalf of the Ways and Means Committee, asking for his reaction to Pell's motion. Harding replied inside the week that he did not think the executive entitled to any tax exemption whatever. The letter, widely noted in the press, proved at once convincing and climactic. It effectively decided the question, and possibly spared the nation the spectacle of an intractable, even demoralizing institutional confrontation. Reportedly, government job seekers calling at the White House on the morning of March 15, the original filing deadline, received a reminder in the virtues of patience while the president checked his prepared return a last time. The *New York Times* chided Harding for his dilatory example.[41]

The troublesome issues gradually reconciled in the Revenue Act of 1921 dealt with gift and luxury taxes, veterans' bonus pay, and exemptions on state-issued bonds, even though the measure contained exactly the same language relating to the presidential salary as the act it superseded. Having accurately read the public mind and gauged the national temper, the president bowed to the intent of the legislative branch. When he quietly approved the bill on November 23, Harding also assessed himself income taxes of more than $18,000 for the year— or fully one-quarter of his official salary. The doctrine of "ability taxation and democratic finance," wrote one optimistic contemporary observer, had been integrated into the nation's revenue program.[42]

The perception proved less incorrect than premature. Harding paid taxes on his salary for the appropriate nine months of 1921 and the whole of 1922, and in the process practically committed his successors to observe the same policy. Certainly Vice President Calvin Coolidge continued it upon Harding's death in August 1923, thereby anticipating the Revenue Act of 1924 and its explicit assertion that the president's salary qualified as gross income under congressional mandate. An enterprising reporter discovered, before the collector barred public access to tax-return files, that Coolidge paid $6,643 for 1923.[43]

At the turn of 1926, however, C. R. Nash, acting Commissioner of Internal Revenue, unexpectedly suspended the evolving precedent. Nash issued a ruling in February, amending Regulation 65, Article 1073, of Section 256 of the Revenue Code promulgated in 1924. Individual tax returns, read the amendment, no longer required divulging information pertaining to "payments made by the U.S.Government to sailors and soldiers and to its civilian employees."[44] This included the president, by logical extension, the *New York Times* reported. Accordingly, the commissioner authorized refund warrants of more than $26,000 to the Harding estate and of an initial $7,000 to Coolidge for the closing five months of 1923.[45]

As before, Congress disputed this interpretation. The Revenue Act of February 26, 1926, repeated the same explicit statement concerning the taxibility of the president's and judges' salaries. In fact, the assertion appeared regularly in each of the Revenue Acts through 1938. The sole omission occurred in 1928, when the Senate failed in its attempt to insert the provision in the usual manner.[46] The Revenue Act of 1932, adopted by the divided Seventy-second Congress, changed the language, possibly in the hope that a less ambiguous rendition, together with a denial of retroactive application, might induce bureaucratic compliance: "In the case of Presidents of the United States and judges of the courts of the United States taking office after the date of the enactment of this Act [June 6, 1932], the compensation received as such shall be included in the gross income; and all Acts fixing the compensation of such President and judges are hereby amended accordingly."[47]

But to no avail. Congress could not lead if the judiciary and bureaucracy refused to follow. Federal judges remained legally exempted by virtue of the Supreme Court's decision of 1920, reaffirmed in 1925, and the president by virtue of the commissioner's order of 1926. Although indications are that Franklin D. Roosevelt met his income-tax obligations, exempting himself only from New York state taxes,[48] he must have puzzled at the confusion. The anomalous condition persisted, not to be harmonized until the impact of the Great Depression altered a variety of traditional institutional relationships.

Several trends converged in 1939 to bring it about. On February 10, the Democratic-dominated Seventy-sixth Congress adopted the first internal revenue bill independent of the historic revenue acts, as if to signal the new importance of income-tax legislation in the nation's finances and affairs. In June, both the president and vice president unveiled the administration's obviously premeditated policy to broaden the taxable base of the population by modifying or eliminating a batch of customary exemptions, starting with the basic individual and married-couples allowances. Meantime, on May 22, the Supreme Court filed its decision in the case of O'Malley vs. Woodrough, declaring that federal judges no longer enjoyed a constitutional protection from refusing to pay national and state taxes on their official salaries. The Court in effect reversed its two earlier judgments, elevating the minority dissent of 1920 to the majority opinion of 1939. Justices Oliver Wendell Holmes, Jr., and Louis D. Brandeis had been vindicated, and the court itself, practically reoriented by the first of Roosevelt's appointments, inclined to attitudes more favorably disposed toward New Deal reforms.[49]

Roosevelt exemplified the permanent transition from the last of the tax-exempted presidents to the first of the fully taxed chief executives of today. It is not clear when the change became legally binding, given the quiet and unpublicized manner in which it was accomplished. It should be noted, however, that the Internal Revenue Code of 1939 contained the final entry in the long reiterated series of congressional dicta on the subject. No such assertion appears in either of the two revisions enacted in 1940. In its place, the Commissioner of Internal Revenue issued amended regulations, with special reference to the judiciary. The operative sentence is cast in a categorical:

"The salaries of Federal officers and employees are subject to [income] tax."[50] Coincidentally, the president's salary had become irrevocably taxable even as the American citizenry was summoned, on the eve of World War II, to discharge the largest single increment in the government's operating budget.

1. *New York Times,* 1 February 1913, 1; ibid., 4 February 1913, 5.

2. *Statutes at Large,* vol. 38, pt. 1, 168.

3. William Howard Taft Papers (Library of Congress, Washington, D.C.), Reel 635, Series 18; Woodrow Wilson Papers (Library of Congress, Washington, D.C.), Reel 502, Series 8J, Tax Returns.

4. Edwin R. A. Seligman, *The Income Tax: A Study of the History, Theory and Practice of Income Taxation* 2d rev. ed., (New York: Macmillan, 1914), 687–88.

5. Richard C. Todd, *Confederate Finance* (Athens: University of Georgia Press, 1954), 140–41.

6. Samuel F. Miller, *Lectures on the Constitution of the United States* (New York: Banis and Bros., 1891), 153–54.

7. Harry E. Smith, *The United States Federal Internal Tax History from 1861 to 1871* (Boston: Houghton Mifflin Co., 1914), 53–54, 61, 73; Carl B. Swisher, *American Constitutional Development* (Boston: Houghton Mifflin Co., 1943), 437.

8. Harry E. Pratt, *The Personal Finances of Abraham Lincoln* (Springfield, Ill., n.p., 1943), 125–27.

9. Collector J. R. Hanna to Joseph Tumulty, February 26, 1914, Wilson Papers, Reel 247, Case 268.

10. Representative Cordell Hull in U.S., *Congressional Record,* vol. 50, pt. 1, April 26, 1913, p. 508.

11. Wilson–McAdoo exchange, February 28, 1914, Wilson Papers, Reel 247; ibid., Reel 502, Series 8J; ibid., Reel 54.

12. Roy G. Blakey, "The New Revenue Act," *American Economic Review* 6 (December 1916): 837–50; Arthur S. Link, *Wilson: Campaigns for Progressivism and Peace, 1916–1917* (Princeton: Princeton University Press, 1965), pp. 60–5; Margaret G. Myers, *A Financial History of the United States* (New York: Columbia University Press, 1970), 278–79.

13. *Statutes at Large,* vol. 39, pt. 1, 758–59; ibid., vol. 40, pt. 1, 329–30.

14. Joshua W. Miles to Joseph Tumulty, April 3, 1918, Wilson

Papers, Reel 502, Series 8J; Memo of 1917, ibid., Reel 502, Series 8H, Investments; Roy G. Blakey, "The War Revenue Act of 1917," *American Economic Review* 3 (December 1917), 805.

15. Richard M. Abrams, "Woodrow Wilson and the Southern Congressmen, 1913–1916," *Journal of Southern History* 22 (November 1956), 435–6; Sidney Ratner, *American Taxation: Its History as a Social Force in Democracy* (New York: W. W. Norton, 1942), 373–8.

16. *New York Times,* 5 October 1917, 1.

17. Ibid.

18. Ibid., 6 October 1917, 1.

19. Ibid., 7 October 1917, 4.

20. Ibid.

21. Ibid., 8 October 1917, 10.

22. Ibid., 4 December 1917, 3; ibid., 19 December 1917, 2.

23. Claude Kitchin, "Who Will Pay the New Taxes?" *The Forum* 60 (July 15, 1918), 149–54; *The Outlook* 120 (November 20, 1918), 446.

24. U.S. House of Representatives, 65th Cong., 2d Sess., *Revenue Bill of 1918,* Report No. 767, September 3, 1918, Serial 7308, p. 9.

25. Ibid.

26. *Congressional Record,* 65th Cong., 2d Sess., vol. 56, pt. 10, pp. 10350–71.

27. Ibid., p. 10350; E. David Cronon, ed., *The Cabinet Diaries of Josephus Daniels, 1913–1921* (Lincoln, Neb.; University of Nebraska Press, 1963), 330.

28. *Congressional Record,* 65th Cong., 3d Sess., Vol. 57, pt. 1: 296, 800; ibid., 57, pt. 3: 2988, 3120; U.S. Senate, *Sen. Doc. 310,* December 6, 1918, Serial 7460, 19.

29. *Congressional Record,* 65th Cong., 3d Sess., Vol. 57, pt. 3: 3137; "Federal Taxation and State Rights," *Constitutional Review* 3 (January 1919), 40–41.

30. Ibid., p. 3035, and Pt. 4: 3271; *New York Times,* 14 February 1919, 12; *Statutes at Large,* vol. 40, pt. 1, 1065.

31. Henry F. Pringle, *The Life and Times of William Howard Taft* 2 vols. (New York: Farrar and Rinehart, 1939), 2, 977–79; Swisher, *American Constitutional Development,* pp. 589–90, 972–73.

32. *New York Times,* 22 September 1918, Pt. 3, p. 1; *The Nation,* 107 (September 21, 1918), 308; William H. Taft, "A $100,000 Salary for the President," *Ladies' Home Journal* 36 (October, 1919), 41–42; Roy G. and Gladys C. Blakey, "The Revenue Act of 1918," *American Economic Review* 9 (June, 1919), 219–20; Edward S. Corwin, "Constitutional Law in 1919–1920," *American Political Science Review* 14 (November, 1920), 641–44.

33. Arthur S. Link, ed., *The Papers of Woodrow Wilson* (Princeton, N.J.: Princeton University Press, 1985) vol. 51, pp. 108–09; W. Elliot

Brownlee, "Wilson and Financing the Modern State: The Revenue Act of 1916," *Proceedings,* American Philosophical Society, 129 (June, 1985), 180.

34. Link, ed., *Papers of Woodrow Wilson,* vol. 41, p. 449; *Wilson Papers,* Reel 502, Series 8J.

35. Carter Glass to Joseph Tumulty, 4 June 1919, *Wilson Papers,* Reel 502, Series 8J.

36. Ibid., Wayne Johnson to John R. Bolling, March 6, 1920.

37. Ibid., Wayne Johnson to Woodrow Wilson, March 8, 1920.

38. *New York Times,* 2 June 1920, 17.

39. Ibid., 5 June 1920, 14; *The Freeman* 1 (June 16, 1920), 313, took strong exception to the ruling, but ignored the implication concerning the president.

40. *New York Times,* 8 February 1921, 5.

41. Ibid., 15 February 1921, 1; ibid., 16 March 1921, 15; *Congressional Record,* 65th Cong., 1st Sess., August 31, 1917, vol. 55, pt. 7, p. 6471.

42. *Statutes at Large,* vol. 42, pt. 1, p. 238; *New York Times,* 2 February 1921, p. 1; Thomas S. Adams, "The New Revenue Act," *The Nation* 108 (March 1, 1919), 316.

43. *Statutes at Large,* vol. 43, pt. 1, p. 267; *New York Times,* 25 October 1924, 2.

44. *Internal Revenue Bulletin* 5 (February 22, 1926), 6–7; *Annual Report of the Commissioner of Internal Revenue,* House Doc. 517, Serial 8744, 38–39.

45. *New York Times,* 21 February 1926, 2.

46. *Statutes at Large,* vol. 44, pt. 2, p. 23; ibid., vol. 45, pt. 1, p. 797; *New York Times,* 6 May 1928, 1.

47. *Statutes at Large,* vol. 47, pt. 1, p. 178; ibid., vol. 48, pt. 1, pp. 686–7; ibid., vol. 52, p. 457.

48. *Literary Digest* 123 (March 27, 1937), p. 7. Pringle, *Taft,* vol. 2, 978–79, contains ex-President Taft's feelings and reactions on the issue.

49. *Statutes at Large,* vol. 53, pt. 1, p. 9; *New York Times,* 14 and 17 June 1949, pp. 1; 307 U.S. 277; Edward S. Corwin, *The President: Office and Powers, 1787–1957* (New York: New York University Press, 1957), 60.

50. *Federal Register,* vol. 5, no. 22 (February 1, 1940), p. 363.

5
Truman and Johnson

The impact of national and state income tax laws upon the presidential salary proved symptomatic of other, largely unnoticed changes occurring during the era. Of course, perquisites and emoluments continued to accumulate, and not merely in the form of facilities, amenities, and technological innovations. The idea of a publicly funded, permanent summer White House or presidential retreat, for instance, gained favor in the 1920s partly with the approval of President Calvin Coolidge. But the salary itself eroded as tax rates rose and proliferated, the cost of living increased, and public expectations mounted. The depression years might have meant enhanced purchasing power, but the presidents, starting with Herbert Hoover, were under growing pressure to acknowledge contemporary conditions and common realities.

The trend became an inherent part of institutionalized life during World War II, and it operates intermittently today. It is particularly evident when a spirit of national sacrifice seems warranted. Concern for the extraordinary federal budget deficits prompted the most recent such gesture. On December 5, 1984, the Reagan Administration proposed "freezing" the fiscal

1986 budget generally at existing 1985 levels in order to slow rising expenditures. In an inducement personally stated the next day, the president volunteered to take a 10 percent cut in his own salary, and called upon the Congress and other high-ranking federal executives to emulate him.[1]

Hoover became the first American president to suffer a real salary reduction. It had to have been his own volition, since the Constitution absolutely precluded it except by the formal process. In 1932, Congress passed an economy bill as part of intensified efforts to arrest the monetary deflation of the deepening depression. A retrenchment device, the measure slashed civil service salaries by 8.3 percent but left most other official salaries untouched. At a meeting in July, Cabinet officers asked the president to subject their salaries to the maximum cut permitted under the new law. This meant $2,250 each for the year, including for the vice president. Hoover then denied himself 20 percent, or a total of $15,000. Only many years later would it be revealed that Hoover, personally a wealthy man, donated the whole of his government salaries, beginning with his confirmation as secretary of commerce in 1921, to charity.[2]

President Franklin D. Roosevelt continued in the manner of the first and most public of Hoover's two precedents, at least for a time, on coming to office in 1933. He voluntarily returned 15 percent of each paycheck to the Treasury through the spring of 1934, while allegedly encouraging an administration publicity campaign against excessive corporate salaries and emoluments. At that point, and over his veto, Congress voted to restore 5 percent of the reduction to civil service salaries. It is not apparent whether Roosevelt reconsidered his position. He may have cooperated by returning only 10 percent, although under no legal constraint to comply.[3]

Much the same practice recurred during World War II, if for opposite reasons. In the interest of promoting patriotic austerity and controlling predictable inflation, Roosevelt issued an executive order in October 1942, erecting a ceiling on large salaries earned by private and public executives. Near the end of the month, James F. Byrnes, director of the Office of Economic Stabilization, published scopious regulations consistent with the presidential directive. There was no mention of the president's salary, but Roosevelt instructed that it not be specially exempted. Therefore, the maximum annual limit of $25,000 established generally also applied to it, after taxes, insurance premiums, and other contracted and fixed liabilities and allowances had been credited. As a result, for example, Roosevelt remitted $1,950 to the Treasury for 1943 in conformity with the guidelines.[4]

Pressures percolated irresistably at the end of the war to relax sweeping emergency controls in favor of returning to traditional free-market determinants. Again, the presidency itself could not but have been effected except through an indirect route, as in the past. President Harry S. Truman's early response was to recommend during a press conference in September, 1945, higher salaries for Congress and civil service personnel. Congressional hearings, begun later in the year, eventually instituted rewards for senators and congressmen, as well as those federal employees who had survived the massive layoffs ordered upon Japan's surrender in August and upon the rapid military demobilization that followed apace. Throughout the proceedings, the president's welfare had been accorded little more than a spurned attempt at revision.[5]

After 1909, a bill to raise the president's salary did not appear again until 1944, between Roosevelt's reelection to a fourth term and his inauguration. A second bill, introduced in December 1945 and devised also to retrieve the income tax exemption and to augment the president's travel allowance, likewise died in committee. Coincidentally, Jonathan Daniels, editor of the Raleigh, North Carolina *News and Observer,* scion of a Cabinet official in the Wilson administration, and himself an advisor to the Roosevelt administration, published an article in a popular news weekly, detailing and dramatizing Truman's financial plight. Two points emerged clearly. The former vice president was hardly a wealthy man, and despite his sudden elevation to illustrious rank, Truman's spendable income, after federal and state taxes had been subtracted and obligatory expenses totaled, amounted to no more than $3,000. The obvious conclusion: The presidency, "the greatest job on earth," left the incumbent "the poorest-paid man in the United States." Nothing immediately came of the publicity, save that the public was treated to a rare spate of historical trivia on the president's salary.[6]

William Howard Taft, a kindly, conciliatory person, chafed under the pressures and demands of the presidency, particularly with Congress in session. But he thoroughly enjoyed the perquisites and privileges then connected to the White House, which facilitated his urge to escape the capital and indulge his predilection for travel. "Congress is very generous to the President," Taft wrote President-elect Woodrow Wilson two months before the inauguration,[7] confessing at the same time that he had saved $25,000 per year of his salary:

You have all your transportation paid for, and all servants in the White House except such valet and maid as you and Mrs. Wilson choose to employ. Your flowers for entertainment and otherwise are furnished from the conservatory . . . .Music for all your entertainments . . . is always at hand. Provision is made by which when you leave in the summer time you may at government expense take such of the household as you need . . . and the expense of their traveling and living is met under the appropriations. Your laundry is looked after in the White House, both when you are away and when you are here. Altogether, you can calculate that your expenses are only those of furnishing food for a large boarding house of servants and to your family, and your own personal expenses of clothing, etc. This of course makes the salary of $75,000, with $25,000 for traveling expenses, very much more than is generally supposed.

Taft, it may be added, typically exhausted the travel allowance, sometimes well before the close of any fiscal year.[8]

These comfortable circumstances may have lasted a time, depending partly on a particular president's personal inclinations and family size, but it seems probable that the salary again proved insufficient by the 1930s. Not surprisingly, Calvin Coolidge banked some portion of his salary, as much as $50,000 per year according to one source, thanks in part to Congress's authorization in 1926 to permit official entertainment to qualify as legitimate expenses under the travel allowance. However, both Herbert Hoover and Franklin D. Roosevelt were forced to draw from private assets in order to meet their costs. Mrs. Eleanor Roosevelt once felt impelled to inform a citizen that the presidency and wealth were scarcely synonymous terms. "I know that as far as my husband is concerned," she confided, "he has spent in fulfilling the obligations of his office . . . somewhat more than his salary"—reportedly, sometimes $175,000 annually.[9]

Pride in the presidency, empathy with its unexpected and unprepared occupant, and postwar inflation all worked in Truman's favor, particularly after his stunning surprise victory in the 1948 elections. A motion in 1946 to salary the president's wife at $10,000 per year failed, among other reasons, for want of competent management and serious preparation. However, the Republican-controlled Eightieth Congress, the famous "do-nothing" Congress which Truman pilloried so successfully on the campaign trail, saw to the codification of Title 3 of the *U.S. Code,* "The President," in the spring of 1948. In the process it provided the president with more than half again the travel allowance previously appropriated, $40,000 at his unhindered discretion, and declared it exempt to taxation.[10]

Soon, too, the idea of permanently attaching a retirement schedule to the presidency found enduring support, together with the older, desultory proposal to acquire an official residence for the vice president. The false start had occurred six years earlier, even as the nation was being drawn into the vortex of World War II. Congressman Robert C. Ramspeck of Georgia and Senator James M. Mead of New York coordinated their parliamentary skills in the Seventy-seventh Congress to enable their colleagues, the vice president, and the president to participate in the civil service retirement system generally available to government workers. The system automatically withheld up to 5 percent of one's salary toward building a retirement fund collectible after a minimum twelve years of service. President Roosevelt approved the act on January 24, 1942, not fully realizing perhaps that elected officials had been partially qualified as federal employees. A surprised and unreceptive public, on learning of the "pension scheme," reacted loudly. Congress quickly repealed the measure amid some grumbling that the press had misrepresented it as an unctious blemish in the spreading blanket of induced and encouraged wartime sacrifices.[11]

A revision in the president's salary came first, with the active assistance of ex-President Hoover. Hoover, having regained something of his tarnished reputation while the appointed head of an executive reorganization study during 1947–49, lent his voice and experience to the cause and, possibly, also to a tax-free expense account. He ably translated the supposedly handsome salary into tangible, easily understood tax obligations and the costs of running the White House as a family residence, which purportedly consumed an average of $2,000 per month. Taken together, according to Hoover, the wonder was that Truman could lay his hands on $1,000 for clothing and mundane family expenses. The press added other details gleaned from anonymous sources. Bess Truman, the president's wife, had tried unsuccessfully to make do with a smaller domestic staff, but had managed to lower food costs by instituting a regime of warmed-over meals. The president, Truman's friends intimated, realized about eighty dollars per week in spendable income.[12]

Truman himself did not hesitate to press the point in his frank midwestern manner when the opportunity finally arose. Asked at a press conference on December 16, 1948, if he would veto a measure to increase the president's salary, Truman told the group of bemused reporters, "I would not. I want you to distinctly understand that I didn't ask for any raise."[13] He explained: "I vetoed the tax bill, which automatically raised my salary. I am not interested in that, but I am interested in the heads of the Government departments receiving a raise in salary, and I think the Vice President ought to have a raise." Truman, like Washington before him, repeatedly expressed concern for the government's ability to attract and retain the services of the ablest, most competent personnel.[14]

With a bipartisan coalition supporting it in the Democratically controlled Eighty-first Congress, buttressed by the handiwork of the Hoover Commission and a mostly friendly press reaction, a comprehensive bill speedily passed Congress, to the benefit as well of the vice president and speaker of the House. By a vote of 68-9 in the Senate and at least two-thirds of the House, the president's salary was increased by one-quarter to $100,000, making it the first revision in forty years. It was also the first revision uncomplicated by an issue in constitutional interpretation. Republican senator Ralph E. Flanders of Vermont, cosponsor of the bill and chairman of the drafting subcommittee, freely acknowledged the influential lobbying of the only living former president, "that sterling New Deal Democrat—ex-President Hoover."[15]

Virtually unanimous support existed in Congress for increasing the president's salary. Criticism centered instead on the merits of adding $50,000 to the standing $40,000 expense and travel allowance and specifying it tax free and unaccountable. As always, it was widely understood, receptions and entertainment cost the president dearly. Not a few agreed with Congressman Ralph E. Church, Republican of Illinois, who called the bill "a fraud on the taxpayers . . . designed as to lead the people to believe that the increase in compensations is merely nominal, whereas in fact the increase is very, very substantial." The bill contained a clever disguise, he contended. It gave the appearance of legislating a total compensation of $150,000, which was reasonably "commensurate with . . . [the] heavy duties and responsibilities." Practically speaking, however, the increase meant the equivalent of $300,000 because nearly half the total was clear profit requiring not even a voucher.[16]

The culprit was Congress itself, according to the critics—that is, the tax exemption passed in 1946. Faced with the usual extraordinary expenses in travel, maintaining two residences, and attendant living costs, Congress voted itself tax-free expense accounts of $2,500 per representative and $10,000 per senator. Now the proposal was to extend the same provision proportionately to the president, vice president, and speaker. It was "a question of principle," the critics protested. "It is wrong to set aside a certain group of Government officials and allow them an income which is not subject to taxes."[17]

Presidential perquisites and gratuities, they noted, were already considerable, excluding the $260,400 lately appropriated to maintain the White House and grounds. Besides, why increase the president's expense allowance when he had spent $8,000 less than the sum provided the previous year? A possible compromise surfaced, based on figures requested of the Internal Revenue Department, to salary the president at $250,000 with no added benefits or emoluments. At current tax rates, he would be left with $112,917 of spendable income. This and other such ideas failed altogether. The momentum to pass the un-amended bill proved unstoppable in the middle of January 1949.[18]

Bitterness and resistance followed in the wake, however. Journalist David Lawrence perhaps best captured the mood in an editorial reprinted in the *Congressional Record*. The "little people," wrote Lawrence, those who voted for the Fair Deal in the last election and to whose interests the administration had dedicated itself, "may not like this."[19]

Truman approved the bill two days after its passage, on January 19. He thanked Congress for its action, but indicated that government salaries still wanted upgrading beyond the three revisions instituted since 1945. In particular, he requested, higher grade officials, including the Cabinet as well as the civil service, generally needed concerted attention. But patience was in order while the House and Senate reconciled their differences on a 538 million appropriations bill that contained the funds destined for the president's and other federal employees' paychecks. With Congress still deadlocked on the bill at the end of April, 1949, Truman to date had received one-third of his newly revised salary and none of the augmented expense allowance. A separate resolution became advisable to authorize continuing the existing salary schedules, which the president reluctantly signed in midMay. Truman started receiving his higher salary four months after the fact.[20]

Crestfallen critics may have been intimidated but scarcely hushed. Republican congressman Roy O. Woodruff of Michigan launched an attack early the next year on "excessive" government spending, citing the president's privileges and perquisites as a prime case in point. According to Woodruff, Truman had been remarkably transformed into "the best paid man in the world." Anyone else would need an income of 3 million dollars annually to emulate the same living standard. For, although the president's "take home" pay after taxes amounted to a defensible $110,000 said Woodruff, also at his disposal were two airplanes, a yacht with standby naval escort, a vacation home in Key West, Florida, a weekend retreat in the nearby Maryland mountains, thirty-five White House limousines and autos, and a private Pullman car. All this necessitated the services of 665 full- and part-time staff whose salaries for the year totaled just under one and a half million dollars. In addition, the president enjoyed the protection of twenty-five Secret Service agents and 107 special police, also charged to taxpayers. (Woodruff carefully refrained from mentioning the five and a half million dollars projected for a comprehensive re-habilitation and expansion of the "third-rate boarding house" the Trumans inherited in April 1945—the White House itself.) Five years later, in 1955, the cost of operating the presidential establishment verged on four million dollars a year—$360,000 more than in Truman's last year, four times more than under Roosevelt in 1944, and seven times more than under either Hoover or Coolidge.[21]

Democratic congressman John W. McCormack of Massachusetts cried foul. Not only had the idea of a presidential salary raise originated in the Eightieth Congress and been supported by a majority of Republicans in the Eighty-first Congress, he noted, but Woodruff had been conspicuous at the time for his silence. Apparently the "little people" rallied, nevertheless. By 1951 a movement had congealed to trim something of the president's advantages. Truman himself helped to galvanize it when he called on Congress in January to authorize ten billion dollars more in taxes, with 40 percent to be taken from personal incomes. The government's current deficits, partly induced by the Korean War, had reached sixteen and a half billion dollars over and above the already large national debt outstanding from World War II. A rumor also circulated that this "largest single tax addition in the history of the Republic" would soon be followed by yet another request for five billion dollars more.[22]

The press turned skeptical. One news weekly seized the opportunity to parade the tensions incited by government officials, themselves proprietors of tax-free expense accounts, embracing legislation designed to weigh down the voters "until it hurts." Those who drafted and passed the laws, it stressed, from the president down to the greenest freshman congressman, simply "do not share the burden equally with the common people." Any "ordinary" citizen, the magazine depicted through bold comparisons and analogies, would have to earn $300,000 annually in order to realize the same after-taxes benefits which the president enjoyed by lawful dispensation.[23]

The "embarrassing" contrast became untenable. In October, the Democratic Eighty-second Congress abolished all such exemptions, including its own individual allowances, effective at the turn of 1953. Since then exemptions of whatever hue and stripe have been anathema. Whereas Truman had paid $56,000 in taxes, incoming President Dwight D. Eisenhower faced yearly obligations of at least $92,000. This left a balance of about $68,000 to live on in the gleaming, completely refurbished White House. Eisenhower behaved stoically, despite having to draw a supposed $25,000 per year from private sources to manage his expenses, while the first lady pored over supermarket sales sheets before dispatching a Secret Service unit with the compiled lists. The president said nothing for the record, even though Truman spoke out on his behalf, roundly insisting that Congress's action had produced consequences neither contemplated nor equitable.[24]

Even so, executive preeminence in national affairs had not lessened appreciably. This was demonstrated, first, by the enactment in 1955 of a modest plan to help maintain the two existing presidential libraries, and secondly, by the adoption in 1958 of a retirement program for ex-presidents and their wives. President Eisenhower quietly approved both measures. The press took little notice of the first one, but sometime since had endorsed the latter. Both of these historic innovations, certainly the action on retirement, owed much to the instigation of former President Truman and his influence upon the leadership of the Democratically controlled Eighty-fourth and Eighty-fifth congresses. The four-room office and secretarial staff Truman operated in Kansas City, Missouri, to manage his correspondence and other public affairs, cost him about $30,000 per year. He doubted he could "keep ahead of the hounds" much longer, he said. "An ex-president is a public figure," one news magazine concluded supportively, "and being a public figure costs money." There was no mention of Truman's pension for his ten years of service in the Senate. The powerful combination of Speaker of the House Sam Rayburn and Senate majority leader Lyndon Johnson also secured Eisenhower's interests upon his retirement in 1961. They were instrumental in having Ike's $25,000 pension and $50,000 allowance as ex-president confirmed, plus his rank as five-star general restored, which he had resigned in 1952 in order to seek the nomination of the Republican party.[25]

The last and most recent salary revision followed ten years later, in 1969. Late in 1967 the Democratic Eighty-ninth Congress, at the behest of the executive branch, passed the Federal Salary Act, authorizing the creation of a specially appointed panel to survey the need for periodic adjustments in the salary structures utilized within the whole of the federal spectrum. President Lyndon B. Johnson named Frederick R. Kappel, retiring head of AT&T, to chair a group which included other prominent corporate leaders and consultants, George Meany of the AF of L, and syndicated financial columnist Sylvia Porter. The so-called Kappel Commission filed its finished report inside the allotted six months, but Johnson took no immediate action on it reportedly because of the Commission's limited advisory character. The report, although never made public, ostensibly recommended "substantial raises" for practically all federal ranks, including the vice president, judges and White House staff.[26]

The administration shortly chose the most direct of two available options. Instead of passing the report to the

Democratic Ninetieth Congress, thereby transferring the initiative to the legislative branch, the administration moved to establish a new, stronger commission under its control. Congress obliged in June, granting the second Kappel Commission powers not only to undertake a systematic review of federal salaries, with its purview automatically renewable at four-year intervals, but also partially binding itself to accept the commission's findings. In December, the administration indicated that the forthcoming budget for the fiscal year, the last one developed under Johnson, would probably recommend general implementation of the Kappel Commission report. Reportedly, the budget would also feature a salary increase for the president. The commission, lacking any mandate to consider the salary, had not spoken to it.[27]

President-elect Richard M. Nixon had been consulted on the pending proposals, according to subsequent revelations. Nixon, the sources divulged, wondered if the sweeping recommendations might not offend public opinion, whereas Johnson thought them still too low. In any event, if Congress agreed, the president's salary stood to be doubled to $200,000 annually. Congressman Carl Albert of Oklahoma, the Democratic majority leader, quickly announced his support. He felt the raise long overdue because every recent president, without exception, had found it necessary to draw on personal savings and assets during his tenure. Truman, Albert had been informed, returned to private life in 1953 "broke."[28]

The House concurred in body, little debating the separate amendment and passing it easily by voice vote after dismissing a demand for a roll call. Majority leader Albert and his opposite, Gerald R. Ford of Michigan, Republican minority leader and cosponsor of the bill in the Democratic controlled Ninety-first Congress, emphasized that the president's salary had been revised a mere four times since 1789, for a total increase of an unimpressive 400 percent. By contrast, even the vice president's salary had risen 860 percent through nine revisions during the same interval. Moreover, Cabinet rank officers had known ten raises and federal judges eleven.[29]

Likewise the Senate approved the amendment by plain voice vote, just hours after the budget plan reached Capitol Hill. Proponents cited current tax rates to help justify the presidential raise, arguing that only $78,000 of the total $200,000 proposed translated into spendable income. The actual increase over the existing salary, therefore, amounted to a paltry $28,000—or what veteran Republican senator Everett Dirksen of Illinois, the chamber's senior wit, labeled "a pretty thin salami." That very evening, at the Longworth House Office Building, Johnson joked at a farewell reception held in his honor that some "question of my judgment and intelligence" had been posed by the fact that after forty years in government, he was "leaving thirteen days before the increase" took effect. More seriously, Johnson commented, "the poor President who will occupy this office for four years will earn every dollar of it, and then some." He signed the bill on January 17, three days before Nixon's inauguration.[30] Scarcely anyone detected the significance of the moment—the presidency had decided to revise its salary by double the former amount and prevailed in having Congress approve the change undiminished and with only modest hesitation.

Once again editorial reaction proved less than favorable. Much of the commentary capitalized on the critics' complaints offered in the House and Senate by Republicans H. R. Gross of Iowa and John J. Williams of Delaware, both of whom suspected the bill functioned as a wedge opening the way to congressional and other salary raises under equally rushed circumstances. Both also wondered at the contradiction involved in doubling the president's salary even as the public had been admonished to help control mounting inflation. Congressman Gross, performing among his last acts before imminent retirement as the taxpayers' putative conscience, cynically observed that none of the candidates had made the president's salary an issue in the late election campaign, and that Congress had conducted no hearings on the matter before opening it to floor debate. Senator Williams, for his part, bemoaned the apparent reversal in priorities. Rather than setting the nation's financial house in order and restoring the value of its currency, the first item on the Ninety-first Congress's agenda dealt with hiking salaries at several prominent levels.[31]

The *New York Times* especially liked Gross's arguments. True, it said, the president's salary needed an upward adjustment, not in the least because of the onerous demands and responsibilities of the office; even at the revised amount, President-elect Nixon stood to suffer "a financial sacrifice in the new assignment." Yet, an increase of 100 percent hardly set the best example when the president's own Cabinet Commission on Price Stability just advised holding raises to 5 percent or less in order to stifle "rampant" inflation. Perhaps, the *Times* suggested, the adjustment might better have come in the form of travel and entertainment allowances instead of "a general increase so big that it will be an inflationary spur in every sector of the economy."[32]

"Inflation by fiat," complained the *New Republic*. The contradiction between the president's raise and the incoming administration's avowed goal of balancing the budget was notable, it said. Even more striking was the "ingenious" new method—the Kappel Commission—by which Congress and practically the entire bureaucracy could pocket sizeable advances—more than 41 percent in some instances—without either applying for or having to vote on them. Total cost: $2.8 billion more per year. "Is this how to fight inflation?" the *New Republic* queried, rhetorically. "You bet it isn't."[33]

The *Wall Street Journal* and *U.S. News* agreed, by implication, after closely examining the president's perquisites and privileges. Noting the next year that the budget plan for the pending fiscal year contained less than nine million dollars for White House staffing and maintenance, a reversal in the contemporary trend, the *Journal* launched its own investigation of direct, indirect, and disguised costs. The *Journal* found, with "detective work and some educated guesses," that the public paid about seventy million dollars per year to sustain the presidency in the style, scope, and decorum to which it had grown. Unnamed references among White House staff called the estimate "too high" but declined to explain. *U.S. News* arrived at a still grander total—$164.4 million—by adding the presumed market value of the White House itself and satellite facilities always at the president's disposal. Regardless, the historic tendency had greatly accelerated since 1960: White House operating costs mounted with each succeeding administration.[34]

The president's salary has not been a matter of any known deliberations since 1969. Two bills were introduced in the House and Senate in late 1974, seeking to cut the salary by 10 percent together with those of either federal workers or congressman, as a salutary gesture toward curbing government expenditures and inflation.[35] Neither proposal won committee approval. Although nearly twenty years have passed since the last revision, the opportunities and conditions favorable to a sixth revision of the president's salary have not been at hand, despite the periodic recommendations of the Commission on Executive, Legislative, and Judicial Salaries. The Watergate episode of the mid1970s and its reverberations, President Nixon's income tax irregularities and audits in particular, focused attention on the presidency in too many refractory ways to be conducive.[36] The monetary inflation of the Carter and Reagan administrations, followed by a steep recession and serious unemployment, comprised patently poor environments in which to propose an upward adjustment. Party allegiances, meantime, have been fractured, shifting or divided, especially between the White House and Congress, probably injecting a further limitation. Concern for the mounting federal budget deficits, moreover, has had the effect of emphasizing the need for restraint. Not only are the benefits and prerogatives extended to ex-presidents coming under criticism and review, but in 1983 the president's salary, because of changes imposed on civil service regulations, for the first time became subject to provisions governing the Social Security Administration. President Ronald Reagan paid the maximum $2,532.60 in obligatory deductions for 1982.[37] The reform is politically, if not legislatively, irrevocable. Once regarded as plenary, insulated and immune to ordinary vagaries, the presidential salary in modern times has been treated increasingly in a manner comparable to that of any other citizen.

Time, events, and socioeconomic trends have made of the salary a symbol of the democratic order. The presidency itself is scarcely ignorant of it. An administration announcement in February, 1985, proposed a 5 percent cut for federal salaries in the pending 1986 budget, potentially the first reduction since the depression. The next day the White House press spokesman made it clear that, if the plan were adopted, President Reagan would voluntarily surrender the same percentage of his salary. The administration plan for major tax reform, unveiled a few months later, received a comparable analysis. The president stood to lose some former deductions, commentators noted, but the loss would be more than offset by the advantage derived from lowered tax rates.[38]

Meanwhile, there are those who would correlate the president's salary to the national median income, render it inversely proportional to the consumer price index, or prohibit any increase except upon public approval as determined by national referendum. Others propose to slash the salary by some significant amount as a start toward cutting the incomes realized by lesser office holders.[39] None of these notions attracts any general support, irrespective of the indifference they suggest to the constitutional stipulation entailed in 1789. Nevertheless, when taken together they confirm that among the many honors and distinctions inherent in the American presidency, the salary beckons the least admiration or envy. It has been the rule for most of the nation's history, certainly for the past century. One recurring view presents the president as an uncrowned king, provided an accrued collection of custom, ritual, and tradition is respected.[40] Perhaps so, but the king must take care to cultivate the common touch and assent to a common salary. That the president's salary will ever become an estimable total seems quite improbable.

1. *Congressional Quarterly* 42 (December 8, 1984), 3062–63.

2. *New York Times,* 16 July 1932, 1; ibid., 24 July 1932, sec. 8, 9; ibid., 29 October 1932, 9; *U.S. News & World Report* 53 (November 26, 1962), 59.

3. *New York Times,* 31 March 1934, 3; Boyden Sparkes, "A Pres-

ident's Salary and Perquisites," *Saturday Evening Post* 209 (November 7, 1936), 22.

4. *New York Times,* 4 October 1942, 22; ibid., 28 October 1942, 1; ibid., 14 January 1944, 11.

5. Ibid., 9 September 1945, 38.

6. Ibid., 1 December 1945, 14; Jonathan Daniels, "That Poor Man in the White House," *Colliers Magazine* 116 (December 1, 1945), 11, 60; *American Magazine* 140 (November 1945), 130; Henry F. Pringle, "Mr. Truman Isn't on the Payroll," *Saturday Evening Post* 219 (August 31, 1946), 6.

7. Arthur S. Link, ed., *The Papers of Woodrow Wilson* (Princeton, N.J.: Princeton University Press, 1978), vol. 17, 16–18.

8. Judith I. Anderson, *William Howard Taft: An Intimate History* (New York: W. W. Norton Co., 1981), 34–36.

9. *Statutes at Large,* vol. 50, pt. 2, p. 305; Henry F. Graff, "The Wealth of the Presidents," *American Heritage* 18 (October 1966), 107—08.

10. *New York Times,* 25 January 1946, 20; *Congressional Record,* 80th Cong., 2d Sess., 1948, vol. 94, pt. 5: 6000–04, and pt. 7: 8822.

11. *Statutes at Large,* vol. 56, pt. 1, pp. 13–17; *New York Times,* 31 January 1942, 12; *Congressional Record,* 77th Cong., 2d Sess., vol. 88, pt. 2: Appendix, A516–17, contains a fair and favorable summary of the bill by Harold Knutson, a Minnesota congressman.

12. *New York Times,* 19 November 1948, 21; ibid., 1 December 1948, 17; John W. Chambers II, "Presidents Emeritus," *American Heritage* 30 (June–July, 1979), 22; *Time* 53 (January 24, 1949), 13–14.

13. *Public Papers of the Presidents,* Harry S. Truman, 1948 (Washington, D.C.: GPO, 1964), 965.

14. Ibid., "Special Message to the Congress on the Need for Raising the Salaries of Federal Executives," June 23, 1949, 326–28.

15. *Congressional Record,* 81st Cong., 1st Sess., 1949, vol. 95, pt. 1, pp. 185–89, 198–222, 414–22, and 666; *The Nation* 167 (December 25, 1948), 711; *Newsweek* 33 (January 24, 1949), 19; *New York Times Magazine* 5 (January 30, 1949); *Time* 53 (January 24, 1949), 13.

16. *Congressional Record,* 81st Cong., 1st Sess., 1949, vol. 95, pt. 1, p. 416.

17. Ibid., pt. 1, pp. 416–17.

18. Ibid., pt. 1, p. 418–20.

19. Ibid., pt. 1, p. 418.

20. *Statutes at Large,* vol. 63, pt. 1, 1949, p. 78; *New York Times,* 6 and 8 May 1929, pp. 17 and sec. 4, p. 12, respectively; ibid., 13 May 1949, 17.

21. *New York Times,* 13 March 1950, 2; *U.S. News & World Report* 39 (July 22, 1955), 30–32; William Ryan and Desmond Guinness, *The*

White House: An Architectural History (New York: McGraw–Hill Co., 1980), 166.

22. *Congressional Record,* 81st Cong., 2d Sess., 1950, vol. 96, pt. 14, Appendix, p. A2214; *New York Times,* 26 January and 3 February 1951, 39 and 1, respectively.

23. *U.S. News & World Report* 30 (February 2, 1951), 26–27.

24. *Statutes at Large,* vol. 65, pp. 569–70; *New York Times,* 2 November 1951, 48; *U.S. News & World Report* 34 (January 16, 1953), 29 and 43–4; ibid. 35 (September 25, 1953), 28–29; Paul A. Carter, *Another Part of the Fifties* (New York: Columbia University Press, 1983), 38.

25. *Newsweek* 49 (February 18, 1957), 33–4; *House Report No. 2200,* 85th Cong., 2d Sess., July 15, 1958, Serial 12075; *Newsweek* 45 (May 16, 1955), 32; *U.S. News & World Report* 39 (July 22, 1955), 30–2; *Life* 42 (March 25, 1957), 42; Chambers, "Presidents Emeritus," 24; Stephen E. Ambrose, *Eisenhower: The President* (New York: Simon and Schuster, 1984), vol. 2, 611.

26. *Statutes at Large, vol. 81, pp. 642–4; New York Times,* 23 March 1967, 17; ibid., 1 January 1968, 30.

27. *New York Times,* 4 June 1968, 43; ibid., 5 December 1968, 32.

28. Ibid., 3 January 1969, 10; ibid., 7 January 1969, 1.

29. *Congressional Record,* 91st Cong., 1st Sess., 1969, vol. 115, pt. 1, pp. 172–73, 174–75.

30. Ibid., pt. 1, pp. 910, 914–15; *Public Papers of the Presidents, Lyndon B. Johnson, 1968–69* (Washington, D.C.: GPO, 1970), 1239; *Statutes at Large,* vol. 83, p. 3.

31. *Congressional Record,* 91st Cong., 1st Sess., 1969, vol. 115, pt. 1, pp. 173–74, 911–12.

32. *New York Times,* 10 January 1969, 46.

33. *New Republic* 160 (February 1, 1969), 10–11.

34. *New York Times,* 29 March 1970, 36; *U.S. News & World Report* 66 (January 27, 1969), 32–34. See also Dan Cordtz, "The Imperial Life of U.S. Presidents," *Fortune* 88 (October, 1973), 145; and Allan L. Damon, "Presidential Expenses," *American Heritage* 25 (June, 1974), 66–67, 94–95, for more systematic efforts.

35. Representative David Martin of Nebraska and Senator Stuart Symington of Missouri in *Congressional Record,* 93rd Cong., 2d Sess., 1974, vol. 120, pt. 26, p. 35552, and pt. 28, p. 37104.

36. John Osborne, *The Fifth Year of the Nixon Watch* (New York: Liveright, 1974), 214–19; John Osborne, *The Last Nixon Watch* (Washington, D.C.: New Republic Book Co., 1975), 51, 107, 168.

37. *New York Times,* 23 March 1984, sec. 4, p. 18; *U.S. News & World Report* 96 (June 4, 1984), 88; ibid., 97 (August 6, 1984), 23–24; *New York Times,* 11 October 1984, sec. 2, p. 10.

38. *Wall Street Journal*, 4 February 1985, 6; ibid., 5 February 1985, 2; *New York Times*, 3 June 1985, sec. 4, p. 5.

39. Editorial, *New York Times*, 3 and 10 February 1974, sec. 4, p. 14, respectively; ibid., 18 February 1977, 26; ibid., 2 December 1980, 18.

40. Michael Novak, *Choosing Our King: Powerful Symbols in Presidential Politics* (New York: Macmillan, 1974).

6
Conclusion

The presidency of the United States, Executive I according to civil service classification, is not a remunerative occupation. It rarely has been. It is not the sort of employment one seeks for its monetary returns. It may be doubted that anyone ever has. The position, if anything, may cost an incumbent funds in addition to the prescribed salary. There is no knowing how many have attested personally to this cold probability, but the total might prove surprising. Regardless, the presidency remains what it always has been, a sacrifice to public service.

Alexis de Tocqueville recognized it in the course of his famous tour through Jacksonian America in the 1830s. He found two types of public employees: those of "secondary rank" whose salaries compared "comfortably" to the people who voted and subscribed them; and the "principal agents," those objects of "excessive parsimony," whose salaries "seem to diminish as the power of the recipients increases." This paradox, among others, de Tocqueville took to evidence the workings of a functioning democracy. For, what a democracy does not pay its leaders and administrators, he discerned, it spends to benefit and assist the people. "In general," de Tocqueville concluded, "democracy gives little to the rulers and much to the ruled."[1]

There is no intent here to comment on the relative adequacy or insufficiency of the president's salary, either historically or contemporaneously. It is not an original observation that there never has been any agreement on the worth of the presidency, if only because any comparison is usually regarded as invidious for one or more reasons. This is not likely to change. Moreover, that the salary falls below possibilities that exist elsewhere remains as obvious today as it became at the turn of the century when Congress conceded the contrast, partly in a mood of bewilderment. There are many salaries in the private sector that range dramatically higher than does the president's, and current comparisons often appear ludicrous despite the last revision in 1969. Rather, the purpose of this study has been to examine the evolution of the president's salary for what it suggests of the institution, its relationship to the Constitution, and the operation of government in a republican system of divided authority.

It may be doubted that the Constitution would have been amended to provide for a presidential salary except that the founding fathers early decreed the office a salaried position. From the first the practice and tendency inclined toward the opposite, to regard the president as the foremost individual among a populace of theoretically equal citizens impelled to the same civic virtues and convictions. The president should be called to public service, it was thought, and answering the call, prepared to serve in the common interest as a concession to duty. However, the founders were also anxious to secure the presidency against rivals' blandishments and encroachments. Their solution, in part, was to guarantee the occupant a compensation and to preclude its being altered during any given term. They could not of course prescribe the amount, nor could they schedule its revisions. They sought only to establish a principle in support of the separation of powers and to decry any play at favoritism or temptation in the form of personal gratuities or enticements.

Yet, practically speaking, the constitutional settlement effectively removed the presidency from actively participating in the determination of the salary. First, any revision tends to occur during the interim between election and inauguration, when much of Congress itself is either disorganized or in transition, and the public is passive or disinterested. Secondly, since by definition a revision must apply to a succeeding presidential term, the incumbent's commitment to it may be on behalf of an administration other than his own. The narrowness of the probable opportunity and the conditional nature of organized support indicates that a broad consensus must be available and basically persuaded as to need. Because this is not often the case, salary revisions have been few and far between and invariably laggard according to any familiar reading of prevailing conditions. This antipathetic practice has resulted in an unintended boon to posterity. Almost every twentieth-century president who survived his tenure earned substantial sums through the publication of autobiographies, memoirs and articles, speaking engagements, and more recently, structured media interviews with contracted rights.[2]

Once fixed, the salary remains so for an indefinite length of time—thus far for not less than twenty years and for an average forty-five years. There is no reason to suppose that the salary revisions of the future will occur any more frequently or regularly than in the past. The influence of certain favorable conditions, it seems, is of greater importance: prosperity, whether real or perceived; a mood of national confidence and well being; and the expectation of desired institutional and socioeconomic reforms. Periods of domestic crisis, as during the Civil War and the Great Depression, apparently are not conducive. Nor are periods of lassitude or complacency, as during the 1820s and 1920s. Foreign anxiety and war, as during the 1940s and 1960s, when the two most recent revisions took place, are not necessarily inhibitory, perhaps because of the strengthened role of executive leadership.

Because of the constitutional settlement, for all realistic purposes, no revision of the salary can occur except that the majority party is strongly supportive of the change and that the president is a member of the same party. It has been the case since 1789, with one notable exception which itself proves the rule. Only in the aborted revision of 1876 were these conditions not met. Opposing parties then controlled the presidency and Congress, so that the proposed revision aimed to reduce, not increase, the salary. This in turn produced a corresponding action, a neutralizing recoil in institutional self-defense. Both an examination and revision of the salary are less products of interparty rivalry than of party dominance, in which members of the minority often lend their support or simply acquiesce. Accordingly, the president in question need not have been elected by a commanding plurality or majority, but he must have been elected. There is no precedent for a salary revision under an unelected president or an accidental successor.[3]

To revise the president's salary successfully is a difficult and occasional occurrence. Popularity alone will not suffice, although it may encourage or contribute to added perquisites. Regular or scheduled revisions appear to be out of the question. A revision depends first on forces converging equal to the building of a reservoir of good will and support. Even then it must be broadly understood that either the incumbent or his legitimate successor is a person of known modest means. Since Washington, all the salary revisions have succeeded because the president or the president-elect were less than wealthy persons. There have been presidents, to be sure, who fit this category and who did not have the opportunity to pass on a revision. Yet, in no instance has a revision been proposed or enacted if a president of recognized or imputed wealth held the office. Not only is it regarded as unseemly, if not improper, for a president publicly to propose a revision, but the presence of a wealthy president may actually serve to suppress any serious consideration. President John F. Kennedy, undoubtedly the wealthiest person to hold the office, let it be known that his paychecks went directly to charity.

Similarly, the president's salary is increasingly debated, if at all, in the context of public servants' salaries more generally. Not since Washington has the salary been treated as a completely separate entity. Its consideration comes not first, but last, usually denoting that an inadequacy has accumulated among a wider range of salaries such that even the president is overdue a revision. Here the president's salary functions as a gauge. Possibly because the Constitution specifically talks to a salary, reference to it is intermittent and when cited, mindful of the stated contraints. Questions impinging upon interpretation and prohibitions become at once predictable and vital. To invoke the constitutional clause thus commonly also serves to signal that a spectrum of official salaries are under review and generally judged to have fallen in arrears. To date, a revision of the president's salary has either been preceded or accompanied by adjustments in other official salaries. No revision of the president's salary has occurred without others also benefiting from the discussion and process.

Conversely, most federal salary considerations,

whether selective or categorical, proceed with a marked indifference to the president's salary. The constitutional stipulation has thus operated to keep the salary nominal and stable over time, and to set it apart from federal salaries as a whole. The standing Commission on Executive, Legislative, and Judicial Salaries, created in 1967, is not independently empowered to contemplate the president's salary. Its recommendations, developed at four-year intervals for all other top government executives except the president, are presented to the White House for acceptance or modification before being sent to Congress for action. Henceforth it is for the president himself to initiate any revision of the salary. President Johnson succeeded in 1969. None of his successors has yet attempted to duplicate the feat.[4] Conditions still operate to render it easier and simpler to augment the perquisites, accouterments, and staffing of the White House, none of which is governed by stated restrictions and much of which may be elicited by the president without violating decorum. These matters are diffused through other, routine budgeting appropriations not necessarily applicable to the executive branch alone. Compiling an inventory of the actual costs of the modern presidency has been virtually impossible, purportedly, since the New Deal reforms of the 1930s.[5]

The result is an anomaly that seems to comport closely to the attitude of the public at large. In general, the attitude permits a liberality toward the institutional presidency, even at the risk of its taking on the appearance and some embellishments of "imperial grandeur." Yet, the attitude also shuns the prospect of the first family either profiting from its entrusted responsibilities or rising to an elitist existence beyond the ken and recognition of the citizenry.

All this helps explain why much of the debate surrounding the president's salary, especially during the twentieth century, has dealt less with current compensation and its equity than with anticipating the status of a once and former president. The president should not receive an exorbitant salary, it is held, yet neither should he find himself compelled to accept prosaic and discomfitted employment after retirement. The tension has been signally ameliorated by the creation of a quasi-official Office of the Ex-President. Indeed, the benefits extended to past presidents since the establishment of a retirement program have been proportionately greater and more easily, sometimes automatically, adjusted. The Former Presidents Act adopted in 1958 portrayed the president as "virtually" unique among federal officials for whom no retirement plan existed. (Congress, in amending civil service regulations in 1956, enabled the vice president to qualify as a member of the legislative branch, to which his salary traditionally had been correlated.)[6] Further, according to the proponents' several justifications, ex-presidents should not be "expected to engage in any business or occupation which would demean the office." To date, five former presidents have been advantaged by the reform, three of whom are yet living. Their privileges, including office facilities, staff, and a variety of expenses in addition to a pension equal to a senior senator's salary, have grown appreciably in the nearly thirty years since enactment. The strongly worded dissenting report one committee filed in 1958, while exaggerated in some particulars, properly noted the generous ambiguities and exceptions contained in the provisions. A recent congressional analysis of the largesse produced mixed reviews tending to sustain the critics' originally ineffectual protest.[7]

Most Americans, although casually aware that the president is a salaried official, are comfortably conscious of and reassured in the knowledge that the actual amount is modest, portends the creation of no aristocratic elite, and is subject to public scrutiny and the same tax laws as are applied to them. The president's special reward is the privilege of residing in the White House and the private enjoyment of its imposing honors, allowances, and perquisites. As every contender knows, the advantages adhering to a president desirous of reelection are impressive and not alone dependent upon superior name identification or the outward trappings of power.[8] In these, Americans have been graciously disposed, even permissive. Instances of complaint have been occasional and usually limited to a particular excess. That immediate financial reward should also ever attend the office, however, beyond those now granted in dignified retirement, appears remote. Today the president of the United States, not unlike most Americans, works for deferred benefits.

1. Alexis de Tocqueville, *Democracy in America,* J. P. Mayer and Max Lerner, eds. (New York: Harper & Row, 1966), pp. 188–89, 197.

2. John W. Chambers II, "Presidents Emeritus," *American Heritage* 30 (June–July, 1979), 18, 21.

3. The observation applies not just to vice presidents who inherited the presidency at the death of an elected president, but also to Gerald R. Ford, who had been elected to neither office.

4. Boyden Sparkes, "A President's Salary and Perquisites," *Saturday Evening Post* 209 (November 7, 1936), 22–23.

5. The commission's most recent recommendations were forwarded to the White House in August, 1985. *New York Times,* 16 August 1985, 1, 28.

6. *Statutes at Large,* vol. 70, p. 760.

7. *U.S. News & World Report* 97 (August 6, 1984), 23–24; *New York Times,* 2 July 1984, 1, 12; Dom Bonafede, "Life after the Oval Office: Caring for Ex-Presidents Can Cost a Bundle," *National Journal* 17 (August 31, 1985), 1943–1947.

8. Richard M. Pious, *The American Presidency* (New York: Basic Books, 1979), 106.

Index

A

Adams, John 15, 16
Albert, Carl B. 86
Aldrich, Nelson A. 41
Austria-Hungary, Emperor of 44

B

Bailey, Joseph W. 43, 44
Bollng, John R. 64
Borah, William E. 42, 45
Bourne, Jonathan, Jr. 41, 44
Brandeis, Louis D. 69
Brodhead, Richard 19
Bryan, William J. 58
Buchanan, James, 44
Buck, Daniel 12–13
Butler, Benjamin F. 20, 27, 28
Burchard, Horatio C. 23
Byrnes, James F. 75

C

Canada, Dominion of 32
Carnegie, Andrew 48
Church, Ralph E. 80
Clark, James B. "Champ" 46
Clay, Alexander S. 42
Cleveland, Grover 36, 40–41, 47, 54
Cockran, W. Bourke 40–41, 46–47

Coit, Joshua 9
Confederate States of America 16, 53
Conkling, Roscoe 30
Coolidge, Calvin 67, 68, 73, 77, 83
Corwin, Edward S. 63
Cox, Samuel S. 26

D

Daniels, Jonathan 76
Dawes, Henry L. 27, 29
Dearborn, Henry 9
Dent, George 13
Depew, Chauncey M. 43
Dillon, Charles H. 59
Dirksen, Everett M. 87

E

Edmunds, George F. 24–25, 29–30
Eisenhower, Dwight D. 84, 85
England, King of 44
Evans, Walter 62, 64

F

Fairbanks, Charles W. 43
Farnsworth, John F. 23
Federal Salary Act 85
Flanders, Ralph E. 80

103

Ford, Gerald R. 86, 102
France, President of 29, 44
Franklin, Benjamin 3

G

Garfield, James A. 20–21, 22,
    25
Germany, Kaiser of 44
Grant, Ulysses S. 20, 22, 24,
    31–32
Great Britain, minister of 29
Gregory, Thomas W. 64
Gross, H. R. 87, 88

H

Hale, Eugene 27, 28
Haiti, President of 44
Hamilton, Alexander 2, 3, 11,
    16, 61
Hancock, John 4
Harding, Warren G. 66, 67, 68
Harper, Robert G. 13–14
Hayes, Rutherford B. 32
Hitchcock, Gilbert M. 46
Hoar, George F. 27
Hobson, Richard P. 47
Holman, William S. 20, 26,
    27, 31
Holmes, Oliver Wendell, Jr.
    69
Hoover, Herbert C. 73, 74, 79,
    80, 83
House, Edward M. 63–64
Howe, Timothy O. 30
Hull, Cordell 58
Huntington, Samuel 4

I

Italy, King of 44
Internal Revenue, Bureau of
    54, 56, 57, 59, 65, 67, 69 81

J

Jefferson, Thomas 15, 16
Johnson, Andrew 53
Johnson, Lyndon B. 85, 86, 87,
    100
Johnson, Wayne 65

K

Kappel, Frederick R. 85–86,
    89
Kasson, John A. 26
Kennedy, John F. 99
Kitchin, Claude 56, 58, 59–60

L

LaFollette, Robert M. 61
Lawrence, David 81
Lear, Tobias 5
Lincoln, Abraham 23, 36,
    53–54
Longworth, Nicholas 59, 66

M

Maclay, William 8
Macon, Nathaniel 14–15
Madison, James 7
Mann, James R. 45
McAdoo, William G. 54
McCormack, John W. 83
McKinley, William 39
Mead, James M. 78

Meany, George 85
Miller, Samuel F. 53

N

Nash, C. R. 67
Nicholas, John 11
Nixon, Richard M. 86, 87, 88, 90

P

Page, Thomas 13–14
Pell, Herbert D., Jr. 66
Penrose, Boies 58
Porter, Sylvia 85
Potter, Clarkson N. 24
President, U.S.
  Libraries Act 84
  Retirement Act 84, 101

R

Rainey, Henry T. 60
Ramspeck, Robert C. 78
Rayburn, Sam 85
Reagan, Ronald W. 90, 91
Revenue Act, 1916 55–56, 61
  1917 55–56, 61
  1918 62, 64
  1921 66, 67
  1928 68
  1932 68
  1940 69
Roosevelt, Edith K. 49
Roosevelt, Eleanor 77
Roosevelt, Franklin D. 68, 69, 74, 75, 77, 78, 83

Roosevelt, Theodore 35–38, 39, 40, 45, 48
Russia, Tsar of 44
Rutherford, Robert 13

S

Salary Grab 21
Sargent, Aaron A. 20, 24, 29
Seligman, Edwin R. A. 52
Smoot, Reed 58
Stanley, A. O. 46
Sulzer, William 47

T

Taft, William H. 48–49, 51–53, 63, 76–77
Thomas, Charles H. 61, 62
Tocqueville, Alexis de 95
Tredwell, Thomas 8
Truman, Elizabeth "Bess" 79
Truman, Harry S. 75, 76, 79, 81–82, 83, 84, 85
Tumulty, Joseph P. 56

U

Underwood, Oscar W. 39
U.S., Articles of
  Confederation 3, 4
U.S. Constitution—
  Article II 3–4, 5, 16, 23, 39, 52–53, 63, 96, 99
  Article III 52–53
  Sixteenth Amendment 51, 52
U.S., Supreme Court 48, 53, 60, 62, 63, 64–65, 66, 68, 69

V

Van Devanter, Willis 62

W

Wadsworth, James W. 58
Wadsworth, Jeremiah 9
Wales, Prince of 29
Warren, Francis E. 43
Washington, George 1, 6, 7,
  10, 12, 40, 79, 99

Williams, John 12
Williams, John J. 87, 88
Wilson, Woodrow 51–52,
  54–55, 56, 62, 63, 64–65, 76
Woodruff, Roy O. 82, 83
Wright, George C. 25, 28